Managing Conflict
and Workplace
Relationships

Managerial Communication Series

By **Sandra D. Collins**
University of Notre Dame

Series Editor: **James S. O'Rourke, IV**
University of Notre Dame

THOMSON
SOUTH-WESTERN

Australia · Canada · Mexico · Singapore · Spain · United Kingdom · United States

AUG 1 8 2004

THOMSON

✦

SOUTH-WESTERN

Managing Conflict and Workplace Relationships, Managerial Communication Series

James S. O'Rourke, IV, series editor; Sandra D. Collins, author

VP/Editorial Director:
Jack W. Calhoun

VP/Editor-in-Chief:
George Werthman

Acquisitions Editor:
Jennifer Codner

Developmental Editor:
Taney Wilkins

Marketing Manager:
Larry Qualls

Production Editor:
Robert Dreas

Manufacturing Coordinator:
Diane Lohman

Production House:
Lachina Publishing Services

Printer:
Transcontinental
Louiseville, Quebec

Sr. Design Project Manager:
Michelle Kunkler

Cover and Internal Designer:
Robb and Associates

Cover Images:
© Artville/Richard Cook

For permission to use material from this text or product, contact us by
Tel (800) 730-2214
Fax (800) 730-2215
http://www.thomsonrights.com

For more information
contact South-Western,
5191 Natorp Boulevard,
Mason, Ohio 45040.
Or you can visit our Internet site at:
http://www.swlearning.com

To my family:
Pam, Colleen, Molly, and Kathleen.
And to my colleagues:
Carolyn, Sandra, Cynthia, and Renee.
Thanks.
JSO'R, IV

To Jarrod and Garett.
And with thanks to Jim and Ron.
SDC

AUTHOR BIOGRAPHIES

James Scofield O'Rourke, IV, is director of the Eugene D. Fanning Center for Business Communication at the University of Notre Dame, where he teaches writing and speaking. In a thirty-five-year career, he has earned an international reputation in business and corporate communication. *Business Week* magazine again named him one of the "outstanding faculty" in Notre Dame's graduate school of business. Professor O'Rourke has held faculty appointments in such schools as the United States Air Force Academy, the Defense Information School, the United States Air War College, and the Communication Institute of Ireland. He is a regular consultant to Fortune 500 and mid-size businesses and is widely published in both professional journals and the popular press.

Sandra Dean Collins currently teaches management communication for the Mendoza College of Business at the University of Notre Dame. Her courses include business writing, speaking, listening and responding, and managing differences. She has also taught statistics and research methods for the university. She conducts team training for the Mendoza College of Business and local organizations and consults with small and mid-size organizations on communication and team-related issues. Her background includes a Ph.D. in Social Psychology and experience in sales, purchasing, and banking.

TABLE OF CONTENTS

FOREWORD

In recent years, for a variety of reasons, communication has grown increasingly complex. The issues that seemed so straightforward, so simple not long ago are now somehow different, more complicated. Has the process changed? Have the elements of communication or the barriers to success been altered? What's different now? Why has communication become more difficult?

Several issues are at work here, not the least of which is pacing. Information, images, events, and human activity all move at a much faster pace than they did just a decade ago. The most popular hip new business magazine is named *Fast Company*. Readers are reminded that it's not just a matter of tempo but a new way of living that we're experiencing.

Technology has changed things as well. We're now able to communicate with almost anyone, almost anywhere, 24/7, with very little effort and very little professional assistance. It's all possible because of cellular telephone technology, digital imaging, the Internet, fiber optics, global positioning satellites, teleconferencing codecs, high-speed data processing, online data storage, and . . . well, the list goes on and on. What's new this morning will be old hat by lunch.

Culture has intervened in our lives in some important ways. Very few parts of the world are inaccessible any more. Other people's beliefs, practices, perspectives, and possessions are as familiar to us as our own. And for many of us, we're only now coming to grips with the idea that our own beliefs aren't shared by everyone and that culture is hardly value-neutral.

For a thousand reasons, we've become more emotionally accessible and vulnerable than ever before. You may blame *Oprah* or *The Jerry Springer Show* for public outpouring of emotions, but they're not really the cause—they're simply another venue for joy, rage, or grief. The spectacle of thousands of people in London mourning the death of Diana, Princess of Wales, took many in the United States by surprise. And after the World Trade Center towers came down in a terrorist attack, few of us had tears left to give. Who could not be moved by images of those firefighters, laboring in the night, hoping against hope to find a soul still alive in the rubble?

The nature of the world in which we live—one that's wired, connected, mobile, fast-paced, iconically visual, and far less driven by logic—has changed in some not-so-subtle ways in recent days. The organizations that employ us and the businesses that depend on our skills now recognize that communication is at the center of what it means to be successful. And at the heart of what it means to be human.

To operate profitably means that business must now conduct itself in responsible ways, keenly attuned to the needs and interests of its stakeholders. And, more than ever, the communication skills and capabilities we bring to the workplace are essential to our success, both at the individual and at the societal level.

So, what does that mean to you as a prospective manager or executive-in-training? For one thing, it means that communication will involve more than simple writing, speaking, and listening skills. It will involve new contexts, new applications, and new technologies. Much of what will affect the balance of your life has yet to be invented. But when it is, you'll have to learn to live with it and make it work on your behalf.

The book you've just opened is the fifth of a series of six that will help you to do all of those things and more. It's direct, simple, and very compact. The aim of my Notre Dame colleague, Professor Sandra Collins, is not to provide you with a broad-based education in either business or communication, but rather to pinpoint the issues and ideas most closely associated with managing both conflict and workplace relationships. Her approach involves far more than dispute resolution or determining how limited resources can be allocated equitably among people who think they all deserve more. She shows us how to manage our own emotions, as well as those of others. Creative conflict, organizational harmony, and synchronicity in the workplace are issues that too many of us have avoided simply because we didn't understand them or didn't know what to say.

In the first volume in this series, Professor Bonnie Yarbrough of the University of North Carolina, Greensboro, examines issues related to *Leading Groups and Teams*. She reviews the latest research on small group and team interaction and offers practical advice on project management, intra-team conflict, and improving results.

In the series' second volume, Professor Carolyn Boulger of Notre Dame explores *e-Technology and the Fourth Economy*. With the help of renowned Swedish communication consultant Hans V. A. Johnsson, she looks at the emergence of a fundamental revolution in how people work, live, and earn a living. And she examines how the new technologies have influenced and transformed everything from commercial relationships to distance learning and more.

Professor Collins, the author of this book who is a social psychologist by training, has also written *Communication in a Virtual Organization*. The conceptual framework she brings to that discussion will help you to understand how time and distance compression have altered work habits and collaboration. With the help of corporate communication executives and consultants, she documents exciting, current examples of global companies and local groups that illustrate the ways in which our work and lives have permanently changed.

For the iconically challenged (I am one who thinks in words and phrases, not pictures), Notre Dame colleagues Robert Sedlack and Cynthia Maciejczyk—with the assistance of a number of well-known artists and graphic technologists—will examine *Graphics and Visual Communication for Managers*. If you've ever wondered how to transform words and numbers into pictures, they can help. And for all of us who've ever tried to explain complex issues without success, either aloud or on paper, the message is simple: If you can't say it in a clear, compelling way, perhaps you can show them.

Finally, Professor Elizabeth Tuleja of the Wharton School of Finance at the University of Pennsylvania will examine *International and Intercultural Communication,* looking both broadly and specifically at issues and opportunities that will seem increasingly important as the business world shrinks and grows more interdependent. As time zones blur and fewer restrictions are imposed on the global movement of capital, raw materials, finished goods, and human labor, people will cling fiercely to the ways in which they were enculturated as youngsters. Culture will become a defining characteristic, not only of peoples and nations but of organizations and industries.

This series of books is interesting, exciting, and highly practical. They're small, of course, intended not as comprehensive texts, but as supplemental readings or as stand-alone volumes for modular courses or seminars. They're engaging because they've been written by people who are smart, passionate about what they do, and more than happy to share what they know. And I've been happy to edit the series, first, because these authors are all friends and colleagues whom I know and have come to trust. Second, I've enjoyed the task because this is really interesting stuff. Read on. There is a lot to learn here, new horizons to explore, and new ways to think about human communication.

James S. O'Rourke, IV
The Eugene D. Fanning Center
Mendoza College of Business
University of Notre Dame
Notre Dame, Indiana

Managerial Communication Series

Editor: James S. O'Rourke, IV

*The **Managerial Communication Series** is a series of modules designed to teach students how to communicate and manage in today's competitive environment. Purchase only this module as a supplemental product for your Business Communication, Management, or other Business course, or purchase all six modules, packaged together at a discounted price for full coverage of Managerial Communication.*

Leading Groups and Teams
Bonnie T. Yarbrough

1 **Managerial Communication Series** | Editor: James S. O'Rourke, IV

ISBN: **0-324-15254-X**

This text, written by Bonnie T. Yarbrough, reviews the latest research on small group and team interaction, and offers practical advice on project management, intra-team conflict, and improving results. It contains group and team worksheets, progress reports, and sample reporting instruments, as well as classroom discussion questions and case studies.

e-Technology and the Fourth Economy
Carolyn A. Boulger

2 **Managerial Communication Series** | Editor: James S. O'Rourke, IV

ISBN: **0-324-15255-8**

This text, written by Carolyn A. Boulger, offers a radical new view of technology's impact on what the author calls "The Fourth Economy," an economic model based entirely on minds in interaction. Technology's role in helping participants in the radically transformed landscape of the twenty-first century is not limited to the transmission and storage of text and data, but extends to the very ways in which people think about and create value.

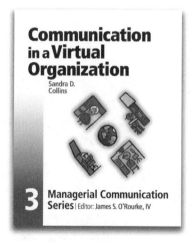

Communication in a Virtual Organization
Sandra D. Collins

3 **Managerial Communication Series** | Editor: James S. O'Rourke, IV

ISBN: **0-324-15256-6**

This text, written by Sandra D. Collins, explores the risks and opportunities open to those who work in new alliances, partnerships, and non-traditional business models. A look at both theory and practical application offers students and managers the chance to observe successful organizations in action.

Contact your local South-Western/ Thomson Learning Representative at 800-423-0563. Or visit the series Web site at **http://orourke.swlearning.com** *for more product information and availability.*

Graphics and Visual Communication for Managers

Robert P. Sedlack, Jr.
Cynthia S. Maciejczyk

4 Managerial Communication Series | Editor: James S. O'Rourke, IV

ISBN: **0-324-16178-6**

This text, written by Robert P. Sedlack, Jr., and Cynthia S. Maciejczyk, offers some practical and useful advice on how to work with graphics and visuals in reports, briefings, and proposals. It also offers direct instruction on how to integrate graphic aids into spoken presentations and public speeches. If you can't say it or write it clearly, you may be able to show it. Dozens of illustrations, drawings, and graphs are included.

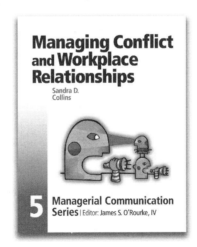

Managing Conflict and Workplace Relationships

Sandra D. Collins

5 Managerial Communication Series | Editor: James S. O'Rourke, IV

ISBN: **0-324-15257-4**

Learn what social scientists and business executives now know about conflict, personality style, organizational structure, and human interaction. This text, written by Sandra D. Collins, examines the most successful strategies for keeping your edge and keeping your friends. Practical forms, instruments, and applications are included.

International and Intercultural Communication

Elizabeth A. Tuleja

6 Managerial Communication Series | Editor: James S. O'Rourke, IV

ISBN: **0-324-15258-2**

This text, written by Elizabeth A. Tuleja, examines the basis for culture, reviewing the work of social scientists, cultural anthropologists, and global managers on this emerging topic. Definitions of culture, issues of cultural change, and how cultures adapt are included, along with practical examples, case studies, and illustrations of how cultural issues are managed both domestically and internationally.

INTRODUCTION

Conflict is a fascinating topic. Granted, when you are caught up in a conflict that seems never ending, "fascinating" might not be the descriptive word you would choose. When we experience conflict directly, we may feel more inclined to describe the situation as unnecessary, perplexing, frustrating, ridiculous, or even as a personal attack. In such settings, it is likely that the other party to the conflict thinks and feels the same way.

The psychology of disputes is equally interesting. We tend to portray disputes as a drama or narrative with a complete cast of characters and actors.[1] We construct these narratives in a way that is cognitively consistent with our view of the dispute. Thus, one way or another, we tend to cast ourselves as the hero. We may be the underdog who is wrongly being attacked, or we may be the ethical person who is taking the principled stand in the face of morally questionable opposition. And, of course, the other side of the dispute gets cast in the role of villain and comes to represent everything that is wrong in our workplace, wrong with our industry, or wrong about the world today. Such stories are polarizing and escalate the situation, making resolution even more difficult to achieve.

The brief story line I present is a familiar one. We have all seen disputes, and we have all experienced conflict directly. We can rest assured we will experience each again—conflict is ubiquitous.

In a recent article in *Strategy+Business,* Joyce Doria and colleagues argue that MBA programs are not doing enough to build the people skills of their graduates.[2] In particular, the authors emphasize interpersonal communication, collaborative skills, and resolving "crises stemming from communication conflicts between cultures" as being the most needed additions to the current MBA curricula. I cite this recent example to illustrate that conflict management skills are important to professionals. Reinsch and Shelby conducted a study at Georgetown University and also found that conflict resolution skills are essential for today's business school graduates.[3] Many more studies illustrating the same point can be found. As organizational hierarchies continue to flatten, as the collaborative demands of knowledge-intensive industries continue to grow, and as we find ourselves working across cultures in an increasingly globalized world, we should expect increased opportunities for misunderstanding, disputes, and outright conflicts. The consequences of increased conflict are clear.

Conflict can be a distracting and expensive issue for managers and organizations. At the interpersonal level, which Professor Collins addresses admirably in this book, conflict can have significant hard and soft costs. Hard costs include time at the office spent worrying or gossiping about the dispute, distractions from duties linked to the organization's strategic objectives, and, of course, clear mistakes resulting from a lack of focus or time. If the dispute moves to a legal front, the costs escalate dramatically. Costs now include the very expensive time of senior management, lawyers, and human resources professionals. We have hard costs associated with discovery, photocopying, faxing, travel, and court fees. And the items just listed are only the hard costs. How do we even begin to measure the soft costs, such as stress and personal health, impact on family, impact on office relationships, and damage to our credibility?

At the organizational level, precisely the same issues emerge. The only difference is that disputes grow larger and more expensive. For these reasons, many business organizations and law firms are collaborating to develop what Michael Landrum calls *conflict control strategies*. Landrum, a lawyer in Minneapolis, Minnesota, who specializes in corporate conflict control, argues that perhaps the most expensive cost of conflict at the corporate level is damage to the company's reputation. Examples of corporate conflict are so numerous that I won't waste your time with anecdotes. Simply open today's *Wall Street Journal* or *Financial Times* and you are likely to find just such a story in print. Instead, the important point is that some companies are starting to view conflict as a strategic issue that can be proactively managed.[4] At the organizational level, corporations are employing the same strategic methods that Professor Collins teaches us in this book. The application is slightly different at the corporate level, but the core strategy is essentially the same.

Conflict remains an always-difficult issue at the national or ethnic level, as well. Recent conflicts in Rwanda or Bosnia-Herzegovina remind us how painful and long-lasting ethnic disputes can be. Additionally, countries like Singapore are viewing arbitration and mediation services as a national opportunity for maintaining regional and economic competitiveness. These countries want to position themselves as regional service centers to which people from many countries travel to take advantage of great healthcare, education, and conflict resolution services. Singapore appears confident that globalization and international business will only increase the need for arbitration and mediation services in Southeast Asia.

Conceptually, we can view conflict at the personal, organizational, and national level. In much the same way, we can also view conflict through different intellectual lenses. Having been trained in conflict resolution in law schools, I have come to look at conflict, mediation, and arbitration through a negotiation lens. From the more legal perspective, we see conflict resolution as a distinct subset of negotiation strategy. Professor Collins takes a useful turn when she approaches conflict from the perspective of social psychology. I think this shift from a legal to social psychological perspective is important and extremely valuable to our understanding of conflict. The shift, in everyday language, is from a perspective about *how we resolve conflict* to the question of *why conflict happens* and *how it works*. I think the how and the why are two sides of the same coin: How can we ever resolve conflict if we don't have some understanding of the dynamics at work? Collins's emphasis on the psychological dimensions of conflict is critical. It is through ideas and models like those presented in this book that you will be able to understand what is happening during a conflict and take meaningful steps to manage or resolve the problem. Taking such decisive action can preserve relationships, reduce unnecessary costs associated with conflict, and allow staff to remain focused on the organization's strategic objectives. Surely this must fall into the category of "an essential managerial activity."

I have no doubt that this book will help you succeed with managing conflict. Professor Collins speaks to the heart of the matter without unnecessary theoretical tangents or in language that requires a dictionary larger than a Tolstoy novel. Instead, what you find in the following pages are models and explanations that help you meet your personal and managerial responsibilities more effectively. Not only can you understand what conflict is and how it operates, but you also receive proven strategies for resolving conflicts, protecting relationships, and more effectively managing some of life's more unpleasant occurrences.

I began this Introduction by suggesting that conflict is a fascinating topic. I hope that after reading this book and successfully applying the ideas presented here, you too are fascinated at how rewarding and exciting it can be to manage conflict effectively.

Michael A. Netzley
Assistant Professor
Singapore Management University

ENDNOTES

1. J. Winslade and G. Monk, *Narrative Mediation: A New Approach to Conflict Resolution* (San Francisco: Jossey-Bass, 2000).
2. J. Doria, H. Rozanski, and E. Cohen, "What Business Needs from Business Schools," *Strategy+Business* 32 (2003): 38–45.
3. L. N. Reinsch and A. N. Shelby, "What Communication Abilities Do Practitioners Need?: Evidence from MBA Students," *Business Communication Quarterly* 60, no. 4 (1999): 7–29.
4. M. Landrum. Available: http://www.mediate.com/burklandrum/, 2003.

1 THE NATURE OF CONFLICT

We are surrounded by conflict in a variety of forms and levels each day. We see an escalation of incivility among strangers and so much personal rage that psychologists have begun to create categories for the various types. Some of this conflict involves us directly, while some we may simply observe. But all of it affects us in some way, just as it affects the organizations we belong to. Though the type of conflict we experience may vary from day to day, one thing remains unchanged: The process is continual and unrelenting. Since the experience of conflict is unavoidable, learning to resolve conflict, or manage conflict that can't be resolved, is essential for all of us.

Robert Ramsey, a contributing editor at *Supervision* magazine, reports that a survey of 150 executives found that they spend an average of about 18 percent of their work time "acting as a peacekeeper, referee, and mediator" for employees engaged in conflict.[1] Other studies estimate that figure to be as high as 30 percent.[2] That means managers are spending between nine and fifteen weeks a year dealing with conflict in the workplace. A recent study by Integra Realty Resources reported that 42 percent of the workers surveyed have witnessed yelling or other verbal abuse at work, and 29 percent of those surveyed admit to having yelled at co-workers themselves.[3] "Sometimes you just snap," explained one Internet company employee who quit his job a week after losing his temper with his boss and letting loose a stream of obscenities.[4]

What's the cause of this increase in workplace conflict? Some contributing factors have been present, at least off and on, for years. An uncertain economy, threats of downsizing, competition for promotion, misplaced loyalties, finger-pointing over mistakes, and job-related stress are all familiar sources of conflict. But the changing landscape at work has brought with it new challenges for keeping peace in the workplace.[5]

- **Rapid pace of business.** Employees are pushed to produce more in less time, creating more stress and short tempers.
- **Increased competition.** Many factors such as technological advances and an increasingly global economy have intensified the competition in numerous markets.
- **Diversity in the workplace.** Organizations strive toward and benefit from greater diversity. With a more diverse workforce, however, comes the difficulty of helping people with different perspectives to get along.

■ **Flattened organizational structures.** Managers and employees are on more familiar terms than they once were, leading to less formal communication. While this has its advantages, it also increases the likelihood that small courtesies and signs of respect may seem unnecessary.[6]

One popular strategy employed by managers for dealing with clashing employees is to wait it out and hope the problem will go away. After all, most managers don't like to interfere in their employees' lives and many feel ill equipped to cope with employee conflict. Interpersonal conflict between employees, however, often doesn't go away by itself. In fact, conflict is more likely to spread as those involved tell others in the organization about it.[8] In one study of how employees respond to conflict at work, more than 86 percent of those surveyed said that they would discuss it with a co-worker.[9] Conversations of this sort can quickly spread conflict through an organization, disrupt harmony and morale in the workplace, and impede work performance.[10]

Conflict Quote ▼

All these different rages—road rage, air rage, whatever rage—are all symptoms of the same thing: We all have too many commitments and too little time.
—Lynne McClure, McClure Associates[7] ▲

Daniel Dana, a mediation specialist and author of *Conflict Resolution*, estimates that 65 percent of performance problems result from conflicts between employees, representing a huge expense for organizations. "Unmanaged employee conflict is perhaps the largest reducible cost in organizations today—and probably the least recognized." Dana encourages managers to examine eight separate factors when estimating the cost of conflicts in their organizations, including wasted time; bad decisions; the loss of skilled employees; restructuring; losses caused by employees through sabotage, theft, or damage; lowered job motivation; absenteeism; and health-related costs.[11]

When conflict begins to affect worker productivity and effectiveness, managers cannot afford to ignore it. They must intervene. While conflicts in the workplace are inevitable, a good leader can plan for them and be ready when they occur. Managing workplace conflict is much like any other managerial skill: It can be learned and developed. An unprepared manager who uses a "wait and see if it gets out of control" strategy for dealing with employee conflict will be ineffective at best.[12] Good preparation involves developing an understanding of conflict, learning ways of analyzing conflicts, and practicing techniques for the resolution and management of conflict, both for yourself and your employees.

COMMUNICATION AND CONFLICT

This book employs a communication approach to understanding and managing conflict. Conflict is inextricably connected to communication. It is through communication that conflict is initiated, expressed, and resolved. Professor Linda Putnam of Texas A&M University conducts research on organizational conflict and negotiation. In her view, "Communication shapes the formation of issues, the emotional climate of conflicts, and the cyclical development of interaction."[13]

What has become clear about conflict and human interaction is that conflicting parties create their conflict experience as they communicate. Early models of communication emphasized the one-way transfer of information from sender to receiver. During the past fifty years, however, these models have evolved to reflect a simultaneously interactive process in which all participants in an interaction send and receive messages at the same time. In this way, each participant influences the messages and the understanding of the other. Thus, the interaction is not simply a delivery system for information but is the process through which meaning is created.[14]

A *communication approach to conflict* suggests that conflicting parties engaged in conflict communication have the power to reshape the current interaction through what they say and do. New communication practices can change experiences and outcomes and can work to transform a negative experience into a positive one. Why is this important? Well, for one thing, it means that one individual can affect change in the conflict interaction. Managers who are caught in a destructive conflict can use different communication practices to move to a constructive conflict. Perhaps even more important, this view means that a manager can effectively intervene in the destructive conflicts of others in the organization by creating change to an element in the system. Just the presence of a manager during an interaction can change the context of the interaction and thereby affect the entire system.[15]

In taking a communication approach to conflict, this book will argue that

- Organizations are social systems with multiple subsystems that are created, maintained, and changed through communication.
- Conflicts are episodes in the ongoing communication processes of the organizational system and subsystems.
- The most effective approach for analyzing conflicts is systemic and includes all known elements in the system.
- The most effective approach for resolving or managing conflict will depend on various systemic factors.
- When the conflict issue and the relationship between conflicting parties are important, the best approach for resolving and managing conflicts will be collaborative communication or dialogue.

The goal of this book is to provide you with an essential understanding of conflict and a working knowledge of the communication tools available for effective conflict management and resolution in the workplace. In this chapter, we introduce the basic concepts of conflict and communication. By the end of the chapter, you will be able to define conflict and describe the process of communication. You will be able to recognize the behavioral consequences of organizational conflict; you will also be able to list major theories of conflict and discuss how they can be applied to analyze and address conflict. In Chapter 2, we'll discuss ways of analyzing conflict, and in Chapter 3, we'll explore techniques for working through conflict.

DEFINING CONFLICT

Conflict may be described in a variety of ways. Popular dictionaries and management texts offer a range of synonyms: (1) to clash, disagree; (2) a battle or struggle; (3) antagonism or opposition; (4) incompatibility or interference; (5) a mental struggle.[16] Each of these definitions describes familiar—and possibly frequent—occurrences, in both our personal and our professional lives.

Social scientists who study conflict often take a more detailed approach to the subject. The recent scientific literature offers these descriptions:

> [C]onflict exists whenever incompatible activities occur. (Deutsch, 1973)[17]

> [Confict is] a situation in which interdependent people express (manifest or latent) differences in satisfying their individual needs and interests, and they experience interference from each other in accomplishing these goals. (Donohue and Kolt, 1992)[18]

> Conflict is the competition between interdependent parties who perceive that they have incompatible needs, goals, desires, or ideas. (Van Slyke, 1999)[19]

> Conflict is an expressed struggle between at least two interdependent parties who perceive incompatible goals, scarce resources, and interference from others in achieving their goals. (Wilmot and Hocker, 2001)[20]

For our purposes, we will use the definition offered by social scientists Wilmot and Hocker. Their definition includes the provision that a struggle between parties be expressed in order to be considered conflict. That expression, however, may not involve raised voices or flying objects. On the contrary, it may be nonverbal and very subtle. In addition, the expression might not be directed toward the other person in the conflict. Frequently, conflicting parties will "vent" to a third party. Not every conflict requires direct, verbal acknowledgment between parties.

Their definition also requires that conflicting parties be, in some way, interdependent. **Interdependence** means that conflicting individuals are, in some important way, dependent on one another. The nature of interdependence varies across relationships. For example, team members on a project team must use each other's expertise to compensate for each individual's gap in knowledge. People or groups can be positively interdependent, meaning that the outcomes will be the same for all. In other words, they will sink or swim together. Alternatively, individuals or groups can be negatively interdependent, where a good outcome for one is at the expense of a good outcome for the other—one swims and the other sinks. Task interdependence is only one form of such interdependence. Members from different organizations may not work together on any tasks, yet they may share the resources available in an office complex. Those shared resources create interdependence. In addition to depending on each other to accomplish tasks, co-workers may depend on each other for social acceptance and emotional support. In a *Fast Company* survey of 1,122 college-educated, working adults, 36 percent of respondents said that they would be friends with their co-workers even if they didn't work together.[21]

Like the nature of interdependence, the degree of interdependence can vary across relationships. In fact, the desired level of interdependence in a given relationship can vary between the

Conflict Quote ▼

Interdependence is a central defining characteristic of work teams because team members, by virtue of their shared responsibility, are dependent upon one another.

—Anne Donnellon, Author of *Team Talk*[22] ▲

involved individuals and can itself become a source of conflict.[23] The degree of interdependence has implications for the risks associated with conflict. Highly interdependent individuals, departments, and organizations are more likely to fear incurring some sort of loss from a conflict.

GOALS

No matter which definition you prefer, it is clear that *conflict begins when one party perceives another party as interfering or potentially interfering with the fulfillment of a need or the achievement of a goal.* The intensity of conflict is related to how much the goal means to the parties involved. A goal is something that someone cares about. There are numerous types of goals, including content goals, process goals, relational goals, and identity goals.[24]

CONTENT GOALS

Content goals involve the choices we make about things that are literally outside of us. Content goals might include such issues as who should receive a promotion, what should be done with an old storage room, or where the company should open a new office. Conflicts about content goals are the result of different ideas about what to do, where to go, who should get what, and the like. Conflicts over these goals almost always involve a perception of scarce resources. People want the same resource, but only one can have it; or they want different outcomes, but only one can happen.[25] For example, if two employees want to be promoted, but there is only one opening, or one partner thinks the new office should be in Dallas while another thinks that Houston is a better choice, content goals are at odds. Conflicts over content goals are very often among the easiest to resolve, although they can become genuinely heated when the goal is especially important to those involved.

PROCESS GOALS

Process goals are about how communication should happen. Conflicts over process goals occur when people do not agree on the type, amount, or depth of communication. In virtually every organization, there are many opportunities for conflict about communication processes and their outcomes.[26] For example, in some organizations the expression of differing opinions may be

---

Conflict Quote ▼

Brad Allen, who is vice president for corporate communication at Imation Corporation, acknowledges a personal dimension to organizational conflict. "Conflict at the interpersonal level," he says, "is frequently driven by style differences or personality differences. One conclusion I've drawn is that direct communication is best, but it must be within the right cultural context—face-to-face, voice-to-voice. E-mail is not the way," he says. "Less mature people begin to feel empowered in an organization," says Allen, especially when they are somewhat removed from those they communicate with. His advice? "Quit the e-mail warfare, the one-upmanship. Walk over, call them, and resolve the issue." Don't let burgeoning egos or a desire to appear tough ruin a good business relationship.[27] ▲

encouraged, while in others that sort of thing may be seen as inefficient or worse. Teams frequently encounter conflict over process goals if norms for processes are not explicitly discussed. Some team members may think that decisions should be made through discussion with all team members. Other members may think that only those with specific expertise on a topic should be required (or allowed) to participate in some discussions.

RELATIONAL GOALS

Relational goals involve how we want others to treat us and how we see our relationships with others. Unlike content goals, which are about something external to the conflicting parties, relational goals are psychological and can often arouse more emotion than content goals. Conflicts over these goals often involve differing expectations between the conflicting parties about their relationship. These conflicts may be about how things should be in the relationship or where the relationship should be going.[28]

Consider, for example, the case of a young woman named Lynn. She was a part-time instructor for a commuter college that served nontraditional students with an accelerated degree program. The campus director who had hired Lynn moved to a different position, and a woman named Ann was brought in as her replacement. Ann met with each of the instructors individually to introduce herself and to get to know them a little. After that initial meeting, Lynn chatted casually with Ann whenever she saw her in the hallway but made no special effort to seek her out for conversation. One day, Ann called Lynn in for a meeting. She expressed disappointment and concern because Lynn didn't talk to her in the same friendly way that she did with students. Ann wondered if there was something wrong between them or if she had done something to keep them from becoming friends. Lynn, of course, was unsettled by the question. She had always viewed her relationship with Ann as professional but not as a potential friendship. To Lynn, everything had been as it should be—until Ann posed that question, which Lynn considered both inappropriate and strange. From that moment on, the relationship between the two women was strained on both sides, with Ann wanting to be friends and with Lynn wanting something a bit different.

In this example, Ann has made her relational goals clear, but many times relational goals are unspoken, making it difficult for people to identify and work through the issues. These conflicts may be initiated or escalated by what one person reads into the words and actions of another and may continue for long periods because the concerns are not openly addressed. Not surprisingly, our relational goals frequently involve self-esteem issues and our interpretation of what other people tell us about our own self-worth.[29]

IDENTITY GOALS

Identity goals are also inextricably tied to our self-esteem. They are about who we believe we are and who other people perceive us to be. Our identities are what we believe to be true about ourselves and are intimately connected to our attitudes, values, and beliefs.[30] Our identity goals, then, can lead to conflict in a couple of ways. First, we may find ourselves in situations in which we feel that we are expected to act in a manner that we see as inconsistent with our identity. Second, we may find that others do not see us as we see ourselves. For example, most people typically don't want others to perceive them as foolish, immature, or weak, and when others do, conflict can result. Conflicts involving identity goals can be intensely emotional.

Identity goals and the desire to preserve and protect identity can become factors in a conflict, no matter how the conflict originally began. Often, we observe people in conflict dig into a losing position and refuse to yield, even when there is clear evidence that they should. They may cling to their position unless an alternative is presented that allows them to "save face" and yield without a threat to their identity. For example, suppose a process engineer considers being an expert in a certain area an important part of his identity. If a process he designed were to be improved by another engineer, he may reject the new design unless it's presented to him in a way that doesn't threaten his identity as an expert.

Even more often than relational goals, identity goals in a human interaction go unspoken. In fact, the participants in an interaction may not be consciously aware that they even have identity goals or that identity issues are providing fuel for an emotionally heated conflict.[31] Consider the story of Rob Peterson, who managed human resources for a software company. Rob was an achievement-oriented person who rarely ever sat still. He was always busy, working toward numerous personal and professional goals. Rob had been talking to his friend Sharon for a year about taking the PHR, a certification exam for human resource specialists. He frequently made statements that began with, "When I take the PHR," yet the study manuals for the exam sat in his office, untouched. One day when he made another reference to taking the exam, Sharon asked him if he really needed to take it. She pointed out that he had been talking about the exam for quite a while but was no closer to being ready for it. Since Rob considered himself to be achievement-oriented, ambitious, and organized, and Sharon's comment suggested that she didn't see him as any of those, it was a threat to his identity. Rob responded to Sharon by slipping into a bad mood but never speaking about the reason or discussing the identity issues related to her comment.

Identity goals can also lead to the avoidance of conflict in cases where the existence of conflict itself is perceived as a threat to our identity. This is most often likely for individuals who achieve much of their identity from a single source.[32] For example, an employee who gains much of his identity—and thus his self-esteem—from having a "great attitude" about his job, may avoid expressing a conflict to his boss. If the conflict issue is serious and threatens the employee's satisfaction with his job, it can become a threat to *who* the employee believes he is as a person, *how* he thinks others see him, and *what* he believes they value in him. With so much at stake, an employee with a vulnerable identity (one that is derived from a single source) is more likely to convince himself that everything is fine than face the threat of conflict.

Conflict Quote ▼

More to the point, work is personal. It helps define who we are. When we find meaning and fulfillment in our jobs, we become more complete human beings.
—*Fast Company*[33] ▲

VALUE GOALS

Value goals are reflected in each of our other types of goals. Our values are what we think is important, right, or good. These values are reflected in our content, process, relational, and identity goals. However, they warrant mentioning separately because they are often at the root of deeply emotional conflicts that we can find confusing. We will sometimes discover ourselves intensely disliking people, not for something they have done to us, but for things they have done or the way they are in general. At times, we may be repelled by entire social groups because we perceive the groups to live by a different code than ourselves, one that violates our values. We may feel an undercurrent of conflict with people we have no obvious interdependence with, but their very nature and existence upsets us. How is this a goal? We have strong, deeply seated reasons for our values and can feel offended (or outraged) when we see others living and behaving in ways that are simply beyond the boundaries of what we think is appropriate.

MULTIPLE GOALS

Multiple goals can be at play in any conflict. Any combination of the four may appear in a conflict, and within any conflict, multiple goals may differ in their relative importance. Goals can also change, develop, and fluctuate in relative importance during the course of conflict. In addition, some goals may be made explicit, while others remain implicit in a conflict.[34]

Keith Magnuson, a software sales manager who occasionally conducts training sessions for new clients, tells the story of arriving early on the day of a training session. Kelly, a training coordinator with the company for seven years, has the responsibility of preparing the training materials. On this particular day, Keith arrived at the office a little early, and the training materials were not yet ready. Renée, Keith's assistant, had been with the company for just two years. She liked her job and her boss and considered Kelly to be a friend. Renée was also in early that day and thought she could be helpful to Kelly and Keith by offering to assemble the materials. When Kelly arrived, she became very upset with Renée for what she perceived as Renée overstepping her role, and let her know it. Renée then complained to Keith. In this conflict, the conflicting parties had different goals and the goals varied in importance. In Figures 1-1 and 1-2, we have diagrammed those goals with circles, representing the importance of the goal by size of the circle.

The nature of the goals can affect the intensity of the conflict. Everyday, garden-variety conflicts may involve only content or process goals, but more serious conflicts usually feature the ego-involving relational or identity goals, or both. The presence of these goals, however, may be hidden behind more obvious and openly expressed content or process goals. A manager, for example, may make changes to an office procedure without discussing it with his assistant. The assistant may be adversely affected by the changes and—had she been consulted—may have been able to offer some suggestions on how to accomplish the manager's goals without all

Figure 1-1   Goals in Conflict: Renée's Goals

Renée was mostly interested in being a nice person and helping out two people she liked. What she was doing didn't matter to her much, so she may not have had important content or process goals.

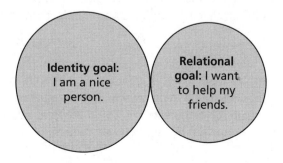

Figure 1-2   Goals in Conflict: Kelly's Goals

Kelly had been with the company for a while and was known to be someone who liked to retain control and to gain recognition for her experience and knowledge about the company. Her primary goal was probably her identity goal.

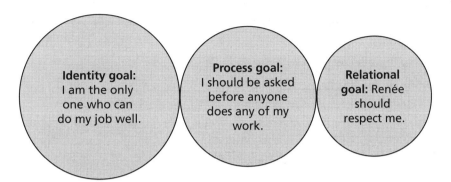

the negative consequences. The assistant may have a conflict over the *content goal* of how the procedure should be written, as well as the *process goal* of not being consulted before changes are made in work she is intimately familiar with. In addition to these problems, the assistant may have conflict over the *relational goal* of having a relationship with her boss based on mutual respect and consideration, and an *identity goal* of being viewed as a valuable contributor of ideas. When and if she confronts her boss about these concerns, she may raise only the content and process goals, explicitly. The relational and identity goals, though, may be even more important to her because of her feelings about her boss and her satisfaction with her job.

Conflict Quote ▼

A New York consulting executive acknowledges that conflict often occurs at more than one level simultaneously: "If it's purely a matter of finances, it's a fairly straightforward discussion," but usually there are underlying circumstances. "It's like the fight you have with your wife," he said. "At one level, it appears to be about that coat she bought but can't afford. And at another level, it's about something else." He paused for a moment and then added: "Look, no relationship lasts forever. You've got to invest in a relationship if it's going to work." That relationship may be personal or it may be professional, but if you want it to last, you may have to change the way you manage the conflict that occurs within it.[35] ▲

THE NATURE OF CONFLICT

Metaphors help people understand their world. Listening to the metaphors of conflict reveal our beliefs about the nature of conflict, how we think it should be treated, and where we believe conflict may lead. In a study of metaphors of interpersonal conflict, the most popular type were animal metaphors (e.g., stubborn as a mule, butting heads).[36] Metaphors of conflict reveal a tendency for attitudes toward conflict to be negative (e.g., conflict is a struggle, a communication breakdown, a trial, a mess).[37]

It's easy to understand why so many people view conflict as a negative experience. Conflict that begins as a simple case of opposing positions can quickly spiral into an exchange of emotionally charged personal attacks. These are **destructive conflicts** and are characterized by verbal and nonverbal insults, ego attacks, inflexibility, a mindset of retaliation, and an exchange of negative emotion.[38]

Conflict Quote ▼

Companies tend to be allergic to conflict—particularly companies that have been in operation for a long time. Being averse to conflict is understandable. Conflict is dangerous: It can damage relationships. It can threaten friendships. But conflict is the primary engine of creativity and innovation.
 —Ronald Heifetz, Director of the Leadership Education Project at Harvard University's John F. Kennedy School of Government[39] ▲

In the past, management has viewed conflict as a negative event to be avoided. But since the 1960s, managers and social scientists have come to recognize the potentially positive aspects of conflict. Traditional views of conflict that blame troublemakers, emphasize legalistic forms of authority, and fail to recognize the importance of conflict have given way to the view that conflict is an integral part of change that can create opportunities for increased trust, relational growth, and joint problem solving. The focus on preventing conflict has given way to the notion that conflict can be *constructive* and there is an optimal level of conflict that is better than no conflict at all.[40] The benefits of optimal levels of **constructive conflict** cited by experts on conflicts in organizations include better decisions and innovative approaches to solving problems. The goal in these organizations is to manage the conflict so that it stays at an optimal level and is not handled in a dysfunctional way.[41] Table 1-1 lists the differences between destructive and constructive conflict.

Recognizing the possible benefits can make it a little easier to accept two realities of conflict. First, conflict is inevitable—even in the best relationships. Since all individuals are unique,

Table 1-1   Differences between Destructive and Constructive Conflict

Destructive Conflict	Constructive Conflict
Increases competition	Increases cooperation
Is mostly emotional	Is mostly cognitive
Involves personal attacks	Separates the person from the problem
Reduces outcome quality	Improves outcome quality
Doesn't solve problems	Solves problems
Weakens relationships	Strengthens relationships
Leads to hurtful behaviors	Leads to personal and professional growth

it is nearly impossible to imagine relationships where people would never have incompatible goals. Conflict isn't a reflection of a dysfunctional relationship or emotional immaturity on the part of those involved. Healthy relationships will experience conflict. The difference between healthy and unhealthy relationships is not whether conflict exists, but how conflict is handled. Second, not all conflicts can be resolved. In some cases, managing a conflict effectively is really the best that you can do.[42]

Conflict Quote ▼

Conflict and disagreement offer wonderful opportunities to learn and grow. As long as you respect others' differences and things don't get personal, as long as you question the idea and not the person, then there will be room for discovery and movement toward the best solution.
—Matthew Gilbert, *Communication Miracles at Work*[43] ▲

While an informed view of conflict acknowledges that conflict can be a positive force, it also recognizes that in many cases that doesn't just *happen*. A positive conflict experience, or a constructive conflict, results from a desire to collaborate rather than compete in resolving the matter. So why don't we see more collaboration and less conflict? Research shows that it's in our nature to compete, even when we could gain more from cooperating. In fact, some social scientists argue that we have a biological drive to compete with each other.[44] Thus, conflict often turns destructive as conflicting parties fail to cooperate. Results from research involving a task known as the Prisoner's Dilemma game has supported the claim that, even when we don't need to compete, we will tend toward a competitive rather than cooperative strategy.[45]

A classroom exercise demonstrates this tendency toward competition. For the exercise, students organize into small groups that represent countries. Each country is asked to make decisions about how many missiles they plan to produce, ranging from zero to six missiles. The groups of students are not allowed to converse with other groups during the decision-making process. However, once they make a decision, they tell a facilitator how many missiles they've decided to produce. The facilitator then provides each country with a reward, typically pennies or candy, for their decision. The size of the reward given to each group depends on the decisions made by that group *and* the others (see Table 1-2). Joint maximum reward is achieved when groups cooperate with each other and choose to produce fewer missiles. The maximum individual reward, however, results from producing more missiles than the other groups.

The process is repeated twelve times. Though the groups are not allowed to communicate directly, they indirectly communicate their desire to cooperate or compete through the decisions they make. Groups can indicate a desire to cooperate by repeatedly choosing to build zero missiles several times even when other groups are competing. However, what usually happens with this exercise is that groups will compete. Research shows that many times, even when a pattern of cooperation has been established between the groups, one group will try a competitive move, which will most likely lead to a competitive retaliation.[46]

The exercise illustrates two important points. First, cooperation is often not the natural tendency for people. Second, getting parties to move from a competitive strategy to a cooperative approach is easier with direct written or spoken collaborative communication. If one person is

Table 1-2   Sample Payoff Matrix for Missile Game with Two Groups

		Number of missiles that Group A chooses to produce		
		0	3	6
Number of missiles that Group B chooses to produce	0	Payoff for both groups is 8.	Payoff for Group A is 6. Payoff for Group B is 2.	Payoff for Group A is 10. Payoff for Group B is 0.
	3	Payoff for Group A is 2. Payoff for Group B is 6.	Payoff for both groups is 5.	Payoff for Group A is 9. Payoff for Group B is 2.
	6	Payoff for Group A is 0. Payoff for Group B is 10.	Payoff for Group A is 2. Payoff for Group B is 9.	Payoff for both groups is 2.

able to say to another person, "If you cooperate, I will too," then cooperation between them is more likely.[47]

The nature of conflict often results in an interplay of motives to compete or cooperate. In laboratory studies of tasks like the Prisoner's Dilemma missile exercise, the goal of the players, to achieve the best payoff, is contrived and not very important to them. The more important the goals, the more mixed the motives of the conflicting parties, particularly if parties are highly interdependent. Competitive motives can sometimes lead to cooperative communication. Conflicting parties may recognize the need to mask their competitiveness with cooperative communication in order to achieve their goals.[48]

BEHAVIORAL RESPONSES TO CONFLICT IN ORGANIZATIONS

Conflicts in organizations can lead to a variety of behavioral responses, many of which are counterproductive for the workplace. The most frequent response to conflict at work is verbalization.[49] People involved in workplace conflict like to talk about it. While they sometimes choose to speak directly to the other party in the dispute about the issue, they very often choose to speak to co-workers outside the conflict, and even to people outside the organization.[50]

Table 1-3   Popular Behavioral Responses to Conflicts in the Workplace

	Direct	Indirect	Uncontrollable
Intensity ↕	■ Discuss with person. ■ Listen to person. ■ Try to convince the person. ■ Shout at the person. ■ Strike the person.	■ Avoid the person. ■ Discuss with co-workers. ■ Discuss with people outside the organization. ■ Talk behind the person's back. ■ Go to the person's supervisor. ■ Make jokes at the person's expense.	■ Show tension nonverbally (clenched jaw, tightened muscles). ■ Cry.

Behavioral responses to conflict can be classified as direct, indirect, or uncontrollable (see Table 1-3). Discussing the issue with the other party in the conflict would be a direct response, secretly sabotaging the other party's work would be indirect, and crying would be uncontrollable (unless tears were produced strategically). Behaviors can also be classified by intensity of response. Avoiding the other party would be at the low end of intensity and striking the person would be at the high end.[51]

In workplace conflicts that continue over a period of time, people engage in numerous behavioral responses as patterns of behavior emerge. Conflicting parties may try one strategy for dealing with the conflict but switch to another if their initial response is ineffective. A common pattern of responding includes switching from some sort of verbalization (e.g., discussing the issue, shouting at the other party) to helplessness (e.g., crying, not talking to the other party, or ignoring the conflict), and back to verbalization.[52] An example of this pattern might be an employee who initially responds to conflict by complaining to co-workers and avoiding the other party in the conflict but eventually raises the issue with the other party directly.

While forms of verbalization and common patterns of responding can allow employees to develop as people and grow their relationships, an increasingly common form of verbalization, due in part to flattened organizational structures and less formal communication at work, includes acts of incivility or rudeness toward others in the workplace. Common examples of rudeness in the workplace include condescending and demeaning comments, overruling decisions without offering a reason, talking about people behind their backs, not giving credit when credit is due, and giving dirty looks. But rude behaviors can become more serious and can include insulting others, yelling, sexually harassing employees, and even becoming violent.[53]

Simple rude behavior is so commonplace it may seem that managers have little choice but to accept it as part of the changing landscape of work. But rudeness and incivility can spiral into a serious conflict, particularly since people have different definitions of what constitutes rude behavior. A thoughtless act that the instigator did not intend to be perceived as rude may be misconstrued and provoke retaliation. Once the original act is reciprocated with an incivility, the spiral begins. A series of reciprocities can lead to escalation. Small acts and little comments can lead to big problems, even acts of violence.[54] Nationally, there are 18,000 cases of nonfatal violence in the workplace per week, and in 2000, some 599 people in private industry were killed as a result of workplace violence.[55]

Coping with rude behaviors at work can have an impact on worker performance. In one study, 53 percent of targets of rude behavior responded by losing time at work worrying, 28 percent lost time at work avoiding the rude person, and 22 percent decreased their effort at work. Organizations can pay the price for their employees' rudeness in other ways, as well. The poor work environment may lead to chronic physical illness in some employees, high levels of turnover, diminished loyalty, and, in some cases, litigation.[56] Workplace violence is now estimated to cost employers from $6.4 billion to $36 billion annually in lost productivity, reputation damage, insurance costs, and increased security.[57]

EMPLOYEE TACTICS FOR DEALING WITH CONFLICT

The behavioral responses of conflicting parties at work are often simply tactics people will use in an attempt to achieve their desired outcomes over time. The tactics employed depend to some degree on the status of the conflicting individuals within the organization. One commonly used tactic is restating a complaint in a new way. If people aren't convincing initially, they may try to rephrase their complaint in a new way that is more effective at achieving the desired outcome. For example, subordinate employees expect statements of fact to receive more attention than personal comments. An employee who doesn't like loud music played in his work area may learn that saying, "The music is distracting" gets more action than saying, "I can't think with that music."[59]

Employees may also learn to raise a complaint about an issue that management will consider important when their true concern is really with an issue that is likely to inspire less of a response.[60] For example, as one company grew, a clerical employee's office was moved to a new office complex that was one large room with numerous Dilbert-style cubicles. The woman was particularly upset by the move because she was a smoker and was able to smoke in her old office, but smoking was not permitted in the cubicles. Instead of complaining about her desire to smoke, the employee raised points about aspects of her job that could be performed more effectively from the old office location.

Employees who feel they are not being treated fairly may resort to a variety of tactics to relieve their frustration, including at times denigrating their manager. They may tell unflattering stories and jokes about the manager or the organization behind the manager's back. Dissatisfied employees may engage in more overt behaviors as well, including pressure tactics. Employees working together, in both unionized and non-unionized organizations, can apply pressure to management by orchestrating slowdowns, absences, and lower product quality.[61]

Because conflict in the workplace is inevitable and, in some ways, even desirable, a manager may have difficulty determining when the nature or intensity of conflict means that intervention is required. Obviously, shouting, threats, or any form of violence will require immediate attention, as does the destruction of property. But behaviors don't have to be this intense to be disruptive to the work environment. When a conflict between two or more employees becomes the "buzz" around the rest of the office, it is probably time to do something. Conflicts that are allowed to continue and aren't managed well can create a tense and uncomfortable environment for employees. Rude behaviors that are disrespectful shouldn't be tolerated. Nor should behaviors that result in slowed performance, like refusing to cooperate or purposely sabotaging efforts.[62]

THEORETICAL APPROACHES TO CONFLICT

A number of theoretical perspectives can offer useful insights into the causes of conflict. Myra Isenhart and Michael Spangle present a summary of current thinking in their book *Collaborative Approaches to Resolving Conflict*.[63] Several of the most important theories for the approach to conflict offered in their book are described next.

ATTRIBUTION THEORY

Attribution theory proposes that people are motivated to make sense of their social worlds so they produce explanations for behaviors that they observe in others and in themselves. Attributions can be **situational** (the behavior is caused by some aspect of the situation) or **dispositional** (the behavior is caused by some aspect of the person performing the behavior).[64] For example, if a co-worker is late to an important meeting with clients, we make a situational attribution if we assume that the cause of the co-worker's tardiness is particularly congested traffic along the co-worker's route to the office. Alternatively, we make a dispositional attribution if we think that the co-worker is late because she is unprofessional and doesn't value punctuality.

Research suggests that people tend to make dispositional attributions when explaining the behavior of others, despite information that highlights the importance of situational influences. In one study that demonstrates this phenomenon, spectators of a quiz show watched while people were assigned by the flip of a coin to the role of questioner or contestant. Those assigned the role of questioner were asked to produce ten difficult questions to ask the contestants. Not surprisingly, the questions reflected the individual questioner's personal store of knowledge, and so the contestants were able to answer only about 40 percent of the questions correctly. After observing the quiz show, spectators were asked to rate the general knowledge level of the questioner and contestant. Even though spectators were aware that roles were randomly assigned and the questions were created by the questioners (so, of course, they knew all the answers), they rated the questioners as having above average knowledge and the contestants as having below average knowledge.[65]

However, exceptions to this tendency to make dispositional attributions do occur. We often make situational attributions if we think that the person we're observing has no choice but to perform a particular behavior or if the behavior is expected in a given situation.[66] For example, if an employee goes outside to smoke a cigarette because the company forbids smoking in the building, we wouldn't infer much about that employee because there is little choice about that behavior. If a supplier picks up the check for lunch with a buyer, we wouldn't attribute that behavior to generosity on the part of the supplier, because picking up the check would be expected in that situation.

As you might well imagine, the type of **causal attributions** that people make for another person's behavior have a tremendous impact on whether conflict will arise and whether or not it escalates or continues. If a colleague doesn't return a phone call or e-mail, we may think that he is rude and irresponsible—or we may think that he must be swamped with work. The explanations that we generate will have an effect on how we respond.

Attribution theory proposes that we observe behavior, make attributions about the causes for what we've seen, and then make inferences about the one performing the behavior. However, we rarely check our attributions and inferences for accuracy. A story shared from the early career years of a former employee of a West Coast bank illustrates this problem. Larry Morrison had been working in operations for two months when he was called into an unexpected meeting with his direct supervisor and the branch manager of his bank. The meeting was about his inability to meet report deadlines. Larry was responsible for preparing and submitting several reports daily, each by a certain time, and he had regularly missed the deadlines since he was hired. His boss was frustrated and felt that, after two months, Larry should be able to perform his job more effectively. She had the option to fire him because he was still in his ninety-day probationary period, but the quality of Larry's work was good, as was his attitude, so she opted to give him a warning and one more chance.

As soon as his boss expressed her concerns, Larry was able to resolve the issue. The supervisor's concerns were the first that Larry had heard about his reports having specific deadlines throughout the day. The person who had trained Larry had done a wonderful job ensuring that he knew how to prepare the reports but never mentioned that they had to be submitted by any specific time. The two managers had inferred from Larry's behavior that he either lacked the ability or the motivation to perform his job effectively. That inference was incorrect, but no one checked on it for two months until the meeting, during which time Larry's performance was below expectations and his supervisor was growing increasingly frustrated. If the supervisor had checked the inference earlier, she could have spared herself a great deal of aggravation and saved the bank the inconvenience and expense incurred from the reports being submitted late.

FIELD THEORY

Field theory proposes that each situation or context creates a psychological field with its own set of forces. The forces of a field will motivate some behaviors and inhibit others. Actual behavior is the result of the interaction between the person and the multiple forces present in the environment acting upon that person.[67] For example, the culture of one organization may consider competition among the sales force a value and demonstrate that value in many ways (e.g., bonuses, contests, awards, expressed expectations, etc.). Even within this sort of culture, other forces, such as friendships among the salespeople, may act to inhibit competition. The competitive behavior observed in any person will be the result of all the forces in the organizational field acting upon that person. In a different context that doesn't value competition, such as one's home, those same employees who exhibit competitive behavior may be extremely cooperative in response to the different forces in the environment. Field theory makes an important contribution to the study of conflict management in that it works against attribution errors by encouraging people to consider situational influences on behavior and conflict.

SOCIAL EXCHANGE THEORY

Social exchange theory takes an economic approach to the understanding of relationships. According to this theory, people are motivated to maximize rewards and minimize costs in relationships and make their choices according to that motivation. Relationships that provide more benefits with fewer costs will be more satisfying. The expectations that people have for relationships, the alternatives they have to that relationship, and the investment that they have already made in it will also contribute to or detract from relational satisfaction and endurance. For example, imagine an employee who starts a new job finds that he enjoys it even more than he expected. He will experience job satisfaction. What happens, however, if he is offered another job that will pay more money than his current position? With this alternative as a comparison, he may experience less job satisfaction. However, if he feels that he has invested a significant amount of time and energy into learning his current job and building friendships with his co-workers, he may remain satisfied with his current job.[68]

EQUITY THEORY

Equity theory is a form of social exchange theory. For the work environment, it involves organizational justice or judgments about fairness in the organization. There are two primary concerns about fairness: one is about the way rewards are distributed, known as **distributive justice**, and the other is about the way things are done, known as **procedural justice**. To ensure distributive justice, organizations and individual managers usually develop norms or rules about how rewards will be allocated. Rewards allocation rules in an organization can be based on equity, equality, or need.[69]

- **Equity-based allocation.** Rewards are distributed according to contribution. A greater reward is given to the person who works harder or contributes more. This is the standard for most North American organizations.
- **Equality-based allocation.** Rewards are distributed equally to all, regardless of contribution. Workmen's compensation is an example of this type of allocation. All employees are covered regardless of their work efforts or job title.
- **Need-based allocation.** Rewards are distributed on the basis of need. Certain grants for MBAs are examples of this type of reward. Only students with a demonstrated need are eligible for them.

Employees will also make judgments about whether the processes used for allocating resources were fair and the procedures were correct. This is known as *procedural justice*. For example, an employee may wonder if, when making decisions about hiring, promotions, or compensation, managers are considering the appropriate criteria and ignoring inappropriate factors (e.g., age or race).[70]

Conflict can result from the perception that resources are not being distributed justly or procedures for allocating resources are unfair. In work situations, perceived unfairness frequently results when employees do not receive the reward they expect. Employees perform a certain amount of work with the expectation that they will receive a certain amount of reward in return. Employee expectations about rewards can be based on previous experience or comparisons with others. In the mid-1990s, Mary Rodino, general manager of voice and data services for AT&T in Chicago, put together a star sales team that called on multi-million dollar clients that had left AT&T and tried to convince them to come back. The team was immensely successful at this difficult task and senior executives wanted to know why. They began looking into the team and found that their commission structure afforded its members more reward than corporate rules usually allowed. As this became known within the organization, sales reps in other divisions were upset and trouble began. The company decided it was time for restructuring. Mary's first thought was, "We've built this amazing team, and not only does the company not appreciate it, but this restructuring is going to destroy it." The team scaled back. Their commissions and bonuses were trimmed. Within a year, one-third of the team members no longer worked for AT&T and, before too long, neither did Mary.[71]

Equity exists when all employees perceive that their rewards are proportional to their contributions, especially as compared with other employees. Inequity exists when an employee feels that the rewards he or she is receiving are somehow different from those that other employees receive for the same amount of effort.[72]

Rewards for employees certainly include salary but also much more. Consider the case of two employees with the same job title, same salary, and same seniority level, but with one employee having a much larger office than the other. The employee with the smaller office may perceive the difference in office size as unjust treatment and become dissatisfied.

An interesting part of equity theory is the assertion that the inequity can be an over-benefit as well an under-benefit, and either of these alternatives will be distressing to the person who perceives it. In our example of the employees with large and small offices, the employee with the larger office may be just as uncomfortable with the arrangement as the employee with the smaller office, if she perceives her larger space as an over-benefit relative to the other employee.

PSYCHODYNAMIC THEORY

Proponents of the **psychodynamic theory** rely heavily on the dynamic forces of the subconscious to explain conflict. Unconscious states can influence perceptions, emotions, and behaviors. These unconscious factors can lead people to behave in ways that are ineffective and even self-destructive. One familiar example of this behavior is *displacement,* in which an employee who is angry at her boss goes home and begins arguing with her husband.[73] Alternatively, a manager who is having difficulty at home may take it out on employees. What is most useful about the psychodynamic theory for our purposes here is its assertion that sometimes conflicts are not about what they appear to be about on the surface.

TRANSFORMATIONAL THEORY

In **transformational theory**, conflict is viewed as an important part of the development of relationships, organizations, and societies. Conflict occurs when there is a perceived discrepancy between how things actually are and how we think things should be. This situation can initiate change and growth. A transformational approach to dealing with conflict doesn't focus on simply finding a solution to the immediate problem, but rather on examining underlying factors and relationships and determining how they are creating and being affected by conflict. The focus is on transforming relationships for long-term benefit.[74]

Food companies are introducing healthier products in response to concerns over consumer health issues, some of which have led to litigation and new labeling requirements. Fast-food restaurants like McDonald's and Burger King have added more salads to their menus, while Hershey Foods Corporation has begun offering sugar-free versions of their most popular candies.[75] Kraft Foods and Unilever Best Foods North America are working to reduce or eliminate the trans fats from its favorite foods while preserving the taste.[76] These organizations are investing in long-term solutions to maintain and improve their relationship with consumers.

SYSTEMS THEORY

The **systems theory** follows that organizations are open, social systems composed of individuals engaged in patterned activities that are interdependent in the process of producing outputs. In general, open systems take resources from outside the system, transform them through the patterned activities of the system, and produce outputs, which are then exported to the environment. Organizations are made up of many subsystems. The organization as a whole and its subsystems refer to patterns of activities. The major components of social systems include their roles, norms, and values. **Roles** refer to the behaviors people are expected to perform when they occupy various positions in the system. **Norms** are the general expectations for how things should be done, and **values** are ideological in nature. These components ensure that activities will be repeated and patterns will develop.[77]

A conflict can occur in a system and lead the system to change. Systems are durable, though, and often resist change. Conflicts can cause systems to become dysfunctional. In organizational settings, systems are functional if they are performing or meeting organizational goals. If a conflict is not managed well, the conflict system can become dysfunctional. People in the system get caught in a pattern of ineffective behavior and keep repeating the pattern, despite its ineffectiveness. Most of us who have worked in large organizations have dealt with dated, ineffective procedures that are slow to change and cause problems in the organization. Another type of breakdown occurs when a part of the system fails or refuses to cooperate. A labor strike is a classic example. Finally, breakdown can occur when a part of the system claims too much power or increases expectations, causing instability.[78]

For most managers, academic theories are only as good as their application to business problems. How can the theories we've described be useful to managers facing conflict in their organization? Each theory offers a different and valuable way of thinking about conflict. Each invites us to consider different aspects of the conflict and ask different questions to help us understand it better (see Table 1-4).

COMMUNICATION AND CONFLICT

Communication is the lifeblood of any organization or any other type of social system. Communication in organizations is the coordinating mechanism that makes accomplishing work possible. The ability to bring resources into the system and export products and services to the external environment depends on it. As a result, both formal and informal communications networks develop to fulfill organizational and individual functions. The patterns that develop define the system and their subsystems. And, when working properly, they help prevent chaos and information overload by restricting the inflow of messages to those that are relevant.

Communication is achieved through a system of interconnected elements, including the sender and receiver of a message, the message itself, the medium selected to deliver the message, and feedback. The entire process occurs within a physical and psychological context. The physical context refers to characteristics of the actual physical setting, such as the size of the

Table 1-4   Summary of Practical Questions Suggested by Each Theory of Conflict

Theory	Question
Attribution theory	Are we making unwarranted inferences about an individual based on his or her behavior?
Field theory	Are there forces in our organizational environment that are encouraging problem behaviors?
Social exchange and equity theory	Are rewards distributed fairly in our organization? Do we show bias or favoritism when we make decisions?
Psychodynamic theory	Is there more at issue here than what there appears to be on the surface?
Transformational theory	How can we make changes that will improve long-term relationships?
Systems theory	What are the identifiable elements and processes that are contributing to this conflict, and which can be changed?

room, the arrangement of the chairs, and the noise level in the hallway. Psychological elements, such as the organizational culture, comprise the context or backdrop within which all communication takes place. Thus, each element in the system contributes to the meaning that is constructed by senders and interpreted by receivers.

From a communication perspective, a conflict is perceived as an episode in an ongoing communication process. Thus, both the process and the outcomes can be changed by a change in any of the elements in the system.[79] If a sender is in a highly emotional state, communication will be affected. A conflict that occurs between people in a particular context, such as a private office, may be completely altered by changing the context to a dinner meeting with others present. If the integrity of a telephone message is compromised by static interference, the entire interaction is affected.

A communication approach to conflicts focuses on the shared construction of meaning that occurs during the communication process. But a common meaning of a message is by no means the guaranteed outcome of the process. Each participant—senders, receivers, and observers—brings his or her own special filters (sometimes called "lenses") to the process, distorting or

Conflict Quote ▼

In organizational systems, meaning-making can be conveyed and derived from language and images, stories and myths, conversational topics or themes, formal documents, acts, objects, rituals, and heroes, as well as orientation and training materials; all of these are created, sustained, and embedded in the formal and informal structure.

—Allan Church, Principal with W. Warner Burke Associates, Inc.[80] ▲

shaping how the message and its content are received and interpreted. *Perception is the process of selecting, organizing, interpreting, and assigning meaning to the information that we receive through our senses.*[81] How we perceive or interpret stimuli in our immediate environment depends on a number of factors, including culture, personality, experience, and mood. Therefore, individual perceptions of the same sensory information can vary tremendously. Jurors who hear the same evidence, for example, will often have very different views of what the evidence means in terms of the defendant's guilt or innocence. Thus, *one message sent to two receivers is really two messages.*

Differing perceptions can be at the root of simple misunderstandings. And all communication is complicated by the fact that we each have our own individual approach to interpreting the messages we receive. In some cases, differences in interpretation can lead to serious misunderstandings. These misunderstandings, however, are really pseudo-conflicts and can quickly be cleared up with effective communication that creates a common understanding of meaning.

It is a myth, however, that all conflicts are about misunderstanding. Frequently, people in conflict are very clear about each other's position, and the positions simply oppose one another.[82] Yet, even in these cases where there is no misunderstanding of the conflicting parties' messages, differences in perception are still important. Consider the story of two project managers.

> *Rick was already feeling the stress of a looming deadline for a project that he considered shaky when the day took a turn for the worse. Jack, who had been Rick's partner on the project, told him about a family vacation he had planned for the following month. Jack explained that he would be leaving immediately after the project deadline, which meant, of course, if anything went wrong and the client asked for changes, Jack would be conveniently out of town, and Rick would have to deal with them on his own. Even worse, he might have to deal with the fallout of a missed deadline. When Rick voiced these concerns, Jack responded with a glib indication of his confidence that Rick "could handle it." Rick was frustrated with what he perceived to be Jack's lack of responsibility and poor work ethic. He was also upset because he considered Jack a friend, as well as a partner, and expected better treatment from him. By the end of the day, Rick let Jack know exactly how he felt in a way that only made things worse.*

The conflict that Rick is experiencing with Jack revolves around differences in their perceptions of the difficulty of the project and Jack's vacation plans. Jack may not share Rick's perception of the project being "shaky" and may think that Rick's concern about last-minute problems and missing the deadline are baseless. Rick, on the other hand, sees Jack's vacation plans as irresponsible and inconsiderate, but Jack most likely doesn't share that perception. Interestingly enough, both managers probably have the same ultimate goal of completing the proposal on time and doing good work, but they differ in how they want to go about achieving that goal. In addition, their definitions of "good work" may not be the same.

Our perceptions will influence our communication, and the way we communicate during a conflict helps shape our perceptions. The way we talk about conflict and the messages we create when we are in conflict will determine the experience we have, as well as the outcomes that are possible. A study performed by Elizabeth Loftus, the psychologist well known for her work on eyewitness testimony, illustrates the profound effect that changing just one word in a message can have on how an event is interpreted and remembered. In her study, participants were shown a film of a car accident in which two cars collide. They were then asked questions about what they saw. Some participants were asked how fast the cars were going when they "smashed" into each other, while others were asked how fast the cars were going when they "hit" each other. Those participants asked the "smashed" question gave significantly higher estimates of speed than those who were asked the "hit" question. Not only did the two groups' interpretation of the event differ in terms of estimated speed, but their memory of the event was affected by the word change, as well. A week after viewing the film, the participants were contacted again and asked if they remembered seeing broken glass at the accident. There was no broken glass in the film, but those who were asked the "smashed" question were more than twice as likely as those who were asked the "hit" question to remember seeing broken glass.[83]

When the perceptions of the messages sent during conflict communication are true to the meanings of the messages, there can still be misperception about what lies behind the messages. In other words, the message could be understood, but the motives, intentions, or logic behind the message could be misperceived. An employee, for example, could perceive a directive from her boss as being restrictive and controlling, while the boss may perceive the directive to be considerate and helpful. This type of misperception can lead to conflicts in which people argue over conclusions based on misperceptions ("You are trying to control me") rather than the behavior that led to the conclusion ("I felt controlled when you gave me that direction"). Often our conclusions contain inferences about other people's intentions. Arguing over conclusions is rarely effective in reaching a solution to conflict for several reasons.[84]

- When we argue our conclusions, the other party has no way of knowing how we arrived at them.
- Arguing our conclusions implies that we have enough information to come to a correct conclusion, but we may not have all the information.
- And, even if we have the same basic information as the other party, arguing our conclusions usually ignores the other party's perspective or interpretation of the information.

People engaged in conflict often become grounded in their own perception, unable or unwilling to take another's perspective. We can have a difficult time widening our span of tolerance to include perceptions that are quite different from our own. This difficulty is in part because, according to our life experience, our perception is correct. It's easy to forget that the other person in a conflict feels the same way about his or her perspective.

Constructive conflict resolution requires learning about the perceptions of others. This is not to say that conflicting parties must agree with the other's perspective, but rather they must demonstrate a willingness and desire to discover what it is. Differing perceptions can play an important role in the initiation and maintenance of conflict, but understanding and tolerating varying perceptions can create opportunities for conflict management and resolution. When conflicting parties begin to understand each other's real interests, this perception may change. And by exploring each other's perspectives and learning what really matters, conflicting parties are often able to generate innovative solutions that allow both parties to satisfy their interests.[85]

Organizations are open social systems composed of multiple subsystems, created through patterns of human interaction. When systems experience an episode of conflict, a change to any of the system's elements will affect the entire system. A communication approach to conflict suggests that changing the patterns of communication will affect the conflict itself. Some conflict is unavoidable, even in the best of relationships, and while communication cannot eliminate conflict, it certainly can work to transform it into a constructive, rather than destructive, experience. Systems, as we've said, can be durable and resist change. In addition, effective communication can be challenging in the best of circumstances. But in a heated conflict where emotions are high, effective communication is even more difficult. Managers need to possess the skills to help them analyze conflict systems and choose the best strategy for managing or resolving conflict.

As you will discover in the remainder of this book, in most cases, a communication approach produces the most desirable outcomes. This is particularly true when the relationship between the parties is important and the issue is of some consequence. And managers who develop and employ the communication tools needed to use such an approach are more valuable to their organizations. In Chapter 2, we will show you how to analyze conflict using a systems approach, considering the important elements in the communication system of conflicting parties. In Chapter 3, we'll explore ways to use communication to work through conflicts and build relationships.

DISCUSSION QUESTIONS

1. Think of conflicts that you have experienced or witnessed in the past. Describe one that turned out to be a constructive conflict for the parties involved.

2. What are some metaphors for conflict not mentioned in the chapter? What do they reveal about your attitudes (and those of others) toward conflict? Create a positive personal metaphor for conflict.

3. Which type of goals do you think are the least likely to be made explicit? Why do you believe this is so? What do you think the effect of this would be on the resolution of conflicts with these goals?

4. Think of a recent conflict that you have experienced. Describe the nature of the goals underlying the conflict. How did that conflict end? Were all the goals discussed during the conflict, or did some remain implicit? If so, which ones?

5. Why do you think more serious conflicts usually involve relational or identity goals?

6. Analyze a recent conflict that you either participated in or witnessed. Which theories of conflict seemed to be involved? How did the conflict play itself out?

7. Recall a time from your own experience when you said something that you regretted saying. What do you think were the effects of what you said?

ENDNOTES

1. Robert D. Ramsey, "Peacekeeping in the Workplace: How to Handle Personality Clashes among Employees," *Supervision,* 58 (1997): 6.
2. Kenneth W. Thomas and W. H. Schmidt, "A Survey of Managerial Interests with Respect to Conflict," *Academy of Management Journal,* June 1, 1976.
3. Robert McNatt, "The List: Desk Rage," *BusinessWeek,* Monday, November 13, 2000, 12.
4. Daniel Costello, "Incidents of Desk Rage Disrupt America's Offices," *The Wall Street Journal,* January 16, 2001, B1, B4.
5. Ramsey, 7.
6. Clive Muir, "Can We All Get Along? The Interpersonal Challenge at Work," *Academy of Management Executive,* 14 (2000): 143–144.

7. Beth Nissen, "Overworked, Overwrought: 'Desk Rage' at Work," CNN.com, November 15, 2000.

8. Patricia Ruzich, "Triangles: Tools for Untangling Interpersonal Messes," *HR Magazine,* July 1999, 129.

9. Roger J. Volkema and Thomas J. Bergman, "Conflict Styles as Indicators of Behavioral Patterns in Interpersonal Conflicts," *The Journal of Social Psychology,* 135 (1995): 5–15.

10. Ramsey.

11. Daniel Dana, "The Dana Measure of Financial Cost of Organizational Conflict." Available: http://www.mediationworks.com, 2001.

12. Ramsey.

13. Linda L. Putnam, "Communication and Interpersonal Conflict in Organizations," *Management Communication Quarterly,* 1 (1988): 295.

14. Steven A. Beebe, Susan J. Beebe, and Mark V. Redmond, *Interpersonal Communication: Relating to Others* (Boston: Allyn and Bacon, 1999).

15. Stephen W. Littlejohn and Kathy Domenici, *Engaging Communication in Conflict* (Thousand Oaks, CA: Sage, 2001).

16. *Webster's Desk Dictionary* (New York: Random House, 1993), 94.

17. M. Deutch, "Conflicts: Productive and Destructive," in *Conflict Resolution Through Communication,* edited by F. E. Jandt (New York: Harper & Row, 1973), 156.

18. W. A. Donohue and R. Kolt, *Managing Interpersonal Conflict* (Newbury Park, CA: Sage, 1992), 3.

19. Erik J. Van Slyke, *Listening to Conflict: Finding Constructive Solutions to Workplace Disputes* (New York: Amacom, 1999), 5.

20. William W. Wilmot and Joyce L. Hocker, *Interpersonal Conflict,* 6th ed. (New York: McGraw-Hill Higher Education, 2001), 41.

21. "Great Expectations," *Fast Company,* November 1999. Available: http://www.fastcompany.com/online/29/greatexp.html.

22. Anne Donnellon, *Team Talk: The Power of Language in Team Dynamics* (Boston: Harvard Business School Press, 1996), 33.

23. Wilmot and Hocker.

24. Ibid.

25. Ibid.

26. Ibid.

27. Brad Allen, Imation Corporation, telephone interview, Oakdale, MN, March 3, 2003.

28. Wilmot and Hocker.

29. Douglas Stone, Bruce Patton, and Sheila Heen, *Difficult Conversations* (New York: Viking, 1999).

30. Stone, Patton, and Heen.

31. Ibid.

32. Wilmot and Hocker.

33. "Great Expectations," 212.

34. William W. Wilmot and Joyce L. Hocker, *Interpersonal Conflict,* 6th ed. (New York: McGraw-Hill Higher Education, 2001), 41.

35. Telephone interview, New York, NY, February 28, 2003.

36. Suzanne McCorkle and Janet L. Mills, "Rowboat in a Hurricane: Metaphors of Interpersonal Conflict Management," *Communication Reports,* 5 (1992): 57–67.

37. Wilmot and Hocker.

38. Ibid.

39. William C. Taylor, "The Leader of the Future," *Fast Company,* June 1999. Available: http://www.fastcompany.com/online/25/heifetz.html.

40. Joe Kelly, "Make Conflict Work for You," *Harvard Business Review,* 48 (1970): 103–113.

41. M. Afzalur Rahim, *Managing Conflict in Organizations,* 2nd ed. (Westport, CT: Praeger, 1992).

42. Beebe, Beebe, and Redmond.

43. Matthew Gilbert, *Communication Miracles at Work* (Berkeley, CA: Canari Press, 2002), 228.
44. Van Slyke.
45. R. D. Luce and H. Raiffa, *Games and Decisions: Introduction and Critical Survey* (New York: Wiley, 1957).
46. Van Slyke.
47. Ibid.
48. William A. Donohue, "Resolving Relational Paradox: The Language of Conflict in Relationships," in *The Language of Conflict and Resolution,* edited by William F. Eadie and Paul E. Nelson (Thousand Oaks, CA: Sage, 2000), 21–46.
49. Roger J. Volkema and Thomas J. Bergmann, "Conflict Styles as Indicators of Behavioral Patterns in Interpersonal Conflicts." *The Journal of Social Psychology,* Vol. 135 (1995): 5–15.
50. Volkema and Bergmann, 5–15.
51. Daniel Dana, *Conflict Resolution* (New York: McGraw-Hill, 2001).
52. Volkema and Bergmann.
53. Pamela R. Johnson and Julie Indvik, "Rudeness at Work: Impulse over Restraint." *Public Personnel Management,* 30 (2001): 457–465.
54. Muir.
55. Carol Elliott, "Safety Policies Can Limit Violence in the Workplace," *South Bend Tribune,* April 7, 2002, B1, B3.
56. Johnson and Indvik.
57. Jennifer Daw, "Road Rage, Air Rage, and Now Desk Rage," *APA Monitor on Psychology,* July/August (2001): 52–54.
58. Nissen.
59. Bruce Fortado, "The Metamorphosis of Workplace Conflict," *Human Relations,* 54 (2001): 1189–1221.
60. Fortado.
61. Ibid.
62. Ramsey.
63. Myra Warren Isenhart and Michael Spangle, *Collaborative Approaches to Resolving Conflict* (Thousand Oaks, CA: Sage, 2000), 4–10.
64. Fritz Heider, *The Psychology of Interpersonal Relations* (New York: Wiley, 1958).
65. Lee Ross, "The Intuitive Psychologist and His Shortcomings: Distortions in the Attribution Process," in *Advances in Experimental Social Psychology,* vol. 10, edited by L. Berkowitz (New York: Academic Press, 1977), 174–221.
66. Edward Jones and Keith Davis, "A Theory of Correspondent Inference: From Acts to Dispositions," in *Advances in Experimental Social Psychology,* vol. 2, edited by L. Berkowitz (New York: Academic Press, 1965), 219–266.
67. Kurt Lewin, *Field Theory in Social Science* (New York: Harper, 1951).
68. Sharon S. Brehm, *Intimate Relationships* (New York: McGraw-Hill, 1992), 157–171.
69. John M. Levine and Leigh Thompson, "Conflict in Groups," in *Social Psychology: Handbook of Basic Principles,* edited by E. Tory Higgins and Arie W. Kruglanski (New York: Guilford Press, 1996), 745–776.
70. Levine and Thompson.
71. Cheryl Dahle, "Don't Get Mad—Get over It!" *Fast Company,* vol. 22, February 1999, 190.
72. E. Walster, E. Berscheid, and G. W. Walster, "New Directions in Equity Research," *Journal of Personality and Social Psychology,* 25 (1973): 151–176.
73. Isenhart and Spangle.
74. Ibid.
75. Sarah Ellison and Brian Steinberg, "To Eat, or Not to Eat," *The Wall Street Journal,* Friday, June 20, 2003, B1.

76. Leila Abboud, "The Truth about Trans Fats: Coming to a Label Near You," *The Wall Street Journal,* Thursday, July 10, 2003, D1.
77. Daniel Katz and Robert Kahn, *The Social Psychology of Organizations* (New York: Wiley, 1966).
78. Isenhart and Spangle.
79. Beebe, Beebe, and Redmond.
80. Allan H. Church, "The Character of Organizational Communication: A Review and New Conceptualization," *The International Journal of Organizational Analysis,* 2 (1994): 18–53.
81. Robert P. Vecchio, *Organizational Behavior,* 3rd ed. (Fort Worth: Dryden Press, 1995), 99.
82. Beebe, Beebe, and Redmond.
83. Elizabeth F. Loftus and John C. Palmer, "Reconstruction of Automobile Destruction: An Example of the Interaction between Language and Memory," *Journal of Verbal Learning and Verbal Behavior,* 13 (1973): 295.
84. Stone, Patton, and Heen.
85. Ibid.

2 ANALYZING CONFLICTS

Conflicts can be confusing to the parties involved and to those observing them. When people are angry or hurt, they often don't understand exactly what's happening in a conflict, let alone know how to resolve it. In fact, people commonly act in ways that make a conflict worse and encourage others to repeat the very behaviors that upset them in the first place. Consider, if you will, a manager who rants and raves whenever he receives bad news from his production supervisor. Furthermore, he complains that his supervisor keeps him in the dark and won't tell him what's going wrong until it's too late to stop it.

Much of our difficulty in understanding conflicts stems from a traditionally employed method of analyzing them, which is *finding fault* and *affixing blame*. In our preceding example, the manager fails to recognize that he contributes to a lack of upward communication by his volatile reactions. Instead, he sees his supervisor as the problem. But conflict is rarely about a "bad guy" who does bad things, so laying blame isn't an effective strategy for conflict analysis. Labeling one person as "the problem" is a counterproductive measure that inhibits any real problem solving. Once someone is given the label, that person becomes the only one with the power to make a change. Others may try to fix "the problem," but no one can *make* another person change. And it's unlikely that "the problem" will agree that all of the fault lies with him and be both motivated and ready to change, or agree to be "fixed" by the others in the conflict.[1]

Instead of rooting out the problem person, systems theory, as described in Chapter 1, encourages analyzing the conflict as a system. This analysis means determining each of the elements in the conflict and how they work together, evaluating individual contributions, identifying dysfunctional patterns, and exploring what purpose the conflict serves within the system. Because a change to any part of the system will create change in the rest, a systems approach expands a manager's options for dealing with conflict. Rather than fixing a problem individual, a manager can try a variety of strategies that target different elements in the conflict, such as changing the context or changing the messages that are sent.[2]

Proposing various solutions is not meant to suggest that any of them will be easy to implement. Changes to a system can be difficult to create. Systems develop their own implicit and explicit rules for how they operate, which can be uncomfortable to break. Consider, for example, the case of a small Midwestern company founded by two friends in the mid-1970s. After decades of growth, one of the founders died. The ownership of the company went completely to the surviving founder, who later retired and turned the business over to his son. The son was not well liked by the managers of the company, who considered him to be incompetent. The managers were frequently in conflict with the son over what the company should be doing and how. In this system, the managers contributed to the ongoing conflicts by following the implicit rule that managers should criticize and joke about whatever decisions the son made. People may continue to follow a system's rules, even if they are dysfunctional for the organization. And when one person decides to change, the others in the system are likely to try to pull that person back into the status quo.[3]

This behavior makes sense because, according to the systems approach, conflict must serve some sort of function for the system or it would not exist.[4] In this example, criticizing the son may help balance the power structure in the organization by allowing the managers to perceive themselves as having more power. This function may be particularly important since the current structure of the company makes it impossible for these managers to move up.

Yet, despite the durability of conflict systems, they can be changed. Maintaining a system requires the willingness of all parties to stay in the roles they occupy within the system. So, if one element of the system changes and is not drawn back into the routine, systemic change will occur. Typically, this change happens not as a result of a management directive to change, but rather from engaging the elements of the system in the process. Thus, we can state a primary principle for a communication approach to conflict management: *Conflict systems are changed through communication between the parties.*[5]

In order to deal effectively with conflict, whether it be their own or that of their employees, managers need a framework to organize the factors that may be contributing to the problem and guide their choice of an appropriate course of action to resolve or manage the conflict. Managers may discover, after a thorough examination of a conflict, that it can be resolved easily without involving the conflicting parties—by procuring more resources or changing a policy, for example. If a manager decides that a conflict issue must be raised with the conflicting parties, preparing by analyzing the conflict before bringing the issue up will make the resolution process go smoother.

In this chapter, we'll discuss various factors that can contribute to conflict. For any given conflict it would be virtually impossible to identify each and every contributing factor, but fortunately that isn't necessary to work through a conflict effectively. We'll look at common contributing factors that are characteristics associated with the elements of the conflict communication system. The elements include the conflicting parties, the messages and the feedback exchanged between the parties, and the physical and psychological context of the conflict. We'll also consider various properties of these elements (see Table 2-1), including levels of conflict, structural and relationship factors, and conflict management styles.

LEVELS OF CONFLICT

Conflict occurs at various social levels and may include intergroup, intragroup, interpersonal, and intrapersonal levels. **Intergroup conflict** refers to conflict between groups. The groups may be very large, such as nations, or much smaller social groups, such as the engineers or the production managers in a manufacturing facility. In organizations, intergroup conflicts can arise between groups at different levels in the organizational hierarchy (vertical conflict) or between groups at the same level (horizontal conflict). When conflict occurs between members of the same group, such as a conflict that occurs within a project team, it is known as **intragroup con-**

Table 2-1   Elements of the Conflict Communication System and Some of their Properties

Conflicting Parties	Physical and Psychological Context	Messages/ Feedback
▪ Level of conflict ▪ Personalities ▪ Conflict management style	▪ Stress ▪ Policies, procedure, norms ▪ Power distribution ▪ Trust	▪ Verbal aggression ▪ Ineffective tactics ▪ Nonverbal cues ▪ Defensiveness

flict and is often about how problems should be solved and how scarce resources should be allocated. **Interpersonal conflict,** or conflict between two individuals, is a concern for many managers because of its frequency. These conflicts can occur between peers or between superiors and subordinates. They can occur between individuals in the same or different departments or even different organizations.[6]

In addition to conflict that individuals may experience with others, people can experience internal conflict, known as **intrapersonal conflict.** Like other levels of conflict, intrapersonal conflicts involve two competing desires or goals, but in this case the desires or goals are competing within the same person. Intrapersonal conflicts take one of several forms: approach-approach, approach-avoidance, and avoidance-avoidance.[7]

Approach-approach. An approach-approach conflict occurs when an individual is attracted to two desirable goals but cannot pursue both. As a simple example, imagine choosing an item from a dessert menu and being torn between the chocolate brownie sundae and the strawberry cheesecake. You want only one dessert but are equally attracted to each of these items. Therefore, you have an approach-approach conflict in which you must choose between two attractive goals.

Approach-avoidance. In an approach-avoidance conflict, an individual is both attracted to and repelled by the same goal. In the preceding example, you could have an approach-avoidance conflict if you were on a diet yet wanted a dessert. Imagine you really want the chocolate brownie sundae, but your diet doesn't allow desserts. You are attracted to the dessert but repelled by the idea of sabotaging your diet.

Avoidance-avoidance. In the case of an avoidance-avoidance conflict, a person is faced with two equally undesirable alternatives. To illustrate this type of conflict, let's change our dessert example slightly. Imagine that you are invited to your boss's home for dinner. After dinner, strawberry cheesecake is served, but you are on a diet and trying to meet your goal of no desserts. In this situation, you have to choose between two undesirable alternatives. You can refuse the dessert, which may be perceived as rude by your boss, or you can eat the dessert and break your diet.

Of course, intrapersonal conflicts are often not as simple as any of the examples just described. Every day we encounter multiple approach or avoidance conflicts in which there are several alternatives, each with positive and negative aspects. As we face these conflicts, we often vacillate between alternatives and may have great difficulty in making and committing to a choice.[8] In fact, any given conflict can become complex, developing at multiple levels. For example, if you know a colleague is acting unethically, you may experience interpersonal conflict with that colleague and intrapersonal conflict as you consider alternative actions to take.

CLASSES OF CONFLICT

In addition to classification by social levels, conflicts can be organized by various typologies with categories that represent the nature of the issue. For example, some conflicts are mostly about cognitive issues (what we know), while others are mostly about affective or emotional issues (how we feel). **Cognitive conflicts,** or **substantive conflicts,** are characterized by arguments about facts, information, ideas, or plans. **Affective conflicts,** or **personalized conflicts,** on the other hand, are much more personal and are characterized by negative emotions, tension, personality clashes, and defensiveness. Cognitive conflicts can be constructive and can produce improved solutions to problems, whereas affective conflicts are more likely to be destructive and damage relationships.[9]

Conflict Quote ▼

While substantive conflict, if handled correctly, can be very productive, personalized conflict is almost never a good thing. There are several reasons. First, personalized conflict is fueled primarily by emotion (usually anger, frustration, and perceptions about someone else's personality, character, or motives).
—Robert Bacal, Institute for Conflict Prevention[10] ▲

Intragroup conflicts are often categorized as task-oriented, process-oriented, or relationship-oriented. Task-oriented conflicts are cognitive in nature, are typically about the work at hand, and do not involve the personalities of the group members. Ironically, task-oriented conflict is the result of group members sharing diverse ideas, which is the very strength of group work. Moderate levels of task-oriented conflict are frequently associated with better outcomes for groups and are, therefore, considered desirable. Process-oriented conflicts, by contrast, are about how things should be done. Both process and relationship conflicts occur at lower levels than task conflict in high-performing teams during a project. And typically, teams that don't perform well tend to show higher levels of task and relationship conflict near project deadlines, suggesting that an approaching deadline may increase stress for teams that are underperforming.[11] Groups that perform well tend to discuss process and don't have to decide over and over how things should be done.

While moderate levels of task-oriented conflict are generally considered desirable for group work, this sort of conflict is clearly beneficial for some tasks and situations and not for others. Research shows that task-related conflict is often helpful with more complex tasks but not with routine tasks. Recent research further suggests that it is not simply the existence or amount of task conflict that improves group outcomes but, more importantly, it's how that conflict is handled. If group members use a constructive approach to their disagreements, then outcomes are improved, but they do not improve otherwise.[12]

Intergroup conflict is often classified as institutionalized or noninstitutionalized. Social institutions are shared ways of doing things. **Institutionalized conflict** is characterized by explicit rules for behavior that set boundaries between groups and legitimize differential treatment of individuals based on group membership. Organizations that support differential treatment of group members—such as restrictions on specialized training or rules about dating clients or fellow employees—would be an example of a system that could lead to institutionalized conflict. In cases of **noninstitutionalized conflict,** members of groups are sometimes treated differently because of their group membership, but the rules for this treatment are implicit and not viewed as legitimate.[13] In North American culture, racism in is an example of noninstitutionalized conflict, and racial discrimination would be an example of differential treatment based on group membership that exists yet is not supported by formal social institutions.

Conflict Quote ▼

According to Kristen Bihary, most organizational conflict is either interpersonal or conceptual in nature. Bihary is vice president for corporate communication at Eaton Corporation, a $7.2 billion diversified industrial manufacturer headquartered in Cleveland, Ohio. She claims, "People put forward competing concepts or ideas, and, if the organization does not specifically understand how to manage conflict, others will react personally rather than professionally or intellectually to what is being proposed."

"Conflict can also arise as a result of the disruption caused by change," she says. Frequently, says Bihary, acquisitions and mergers will cause the greatest stress in an organization as it tries to establish a single culture for all employees.

Avoiding conflict, in her view, is not a good idea. "You don't get anywhere by holding back or holding in." Many organizations, according to Bihary, are really passive/aggressive in nature. The reason? "Many people don't like confrontation. They don't like telling other people 'no.' You think you have agreement on an issue or course of action and head off in that direction," she says. "Later you find out you didn't have agreement at all. The result is inefficiency at best and disaster at worst."[14] ▲

FACTORS CONTRIBUTING TO CONFLICT IN THE WORKPLACE

Numerous factors contribute to conflict in the workplace. Some are very specific to certain industries, organizations, groups, or individuals, while some are common to all workplace situations. In this section, we will discuss contributing factors that are present in work environments across all industries and organizations. We'll begin by discussing general factors that have an impact at all levels of conflict, including structural factors existing outside of the conflicting parties and relational factors that have to do with the parties themselves. Then, we'll take up the factors that contribute at specific levels of conflict.

PHYSICAL CONTEXT: STRUCTURAL FACTORS

Structural factors are situational. They exist apart from the individuals who are exposed to them, and they tend to affect most people in similar ways. As we noted in Chapter 1, the contribution of situational factors is often undervalued when we attempt to explain people's behavior. When we analyze conflicts, we must be cautious about committing this attribution error. Sometimes conflict is rooted in situational factors. At times, the conflict can be resolved by changing the situation, without ever bringing the conflicting parties together or raising the issue with either of them. Each conflict will present its own unique, situational variables for us to consider as we analyze the problem. For now, we'll review just a handful of the most common situational contributors to conflict.

STRESS

Without question, the number one contributor to conflict in the workplace today is work-related **stress.** One in every ten U.S. workers considers job stress a major problem, and 30 percent of Americans actually lose sleep from work-related stress.[15] Stress is a psychological and physiological reaction to what we perceive to be a threat in our environment. A common source of stress today is the need to accomplish many tasks in a short period of time. Phil, a controller, shares an example. As an accountant, he is responsible for preparing numerous monthly reports during a limited time span. Periodically, he experiences a great deal of stress as he tries to complete the reports while dealing with repeated interruptions that distract him from the task. The threat he faces is not completing his reports by the time his supervisor needs them.

A certain amount of stress or pressure, like that from an approaching deadline, is often what energizes people to get things done. The problem with stress is that the human response to it hasn't changed over time, even though the demands of our environment have. We still respond to stress with the fight-or-flight reaction, which may have been appropriate when the threats we faced were wild animals or raiding marauders, but it is not particularly useful for the kinds of stressful situations we typically encounter today. In stressful situations, we continue to have a physical response, but today's situations usually require a mental solution. While we do occasionally see people respond to an unresponsive computer by hitting it or to an uncooperative vending machine by kicking it, those reactions are usually ineffective for coping with our workplace stressors.

Though these physical outbursts aren't really effective, the stress response releases chemicals into our systems to prepare us for physical activity. Frequently experiencing the stress response without any corresponding physical exertion can lead to serious health problems. We have long heard about the unhealthy consequences of chronic stress, including headaches, fatigue, rashes, digestive disorders, hypertension, and heart disease. For our purposes, another important consequence of stress is the effect it has on our ability to communicate well. The irritability or short fuse that is so pervasive in today's workforce is a major contributor to workplace conflict.

> **Conflict Quote ▼**
>
> *Stress is one of many potential triggers for aggressive responses in the workplace.*
> —Susan Burroughs, Roosevelt University[16] ▲

What are the causes of stress in the workplace? If you have worked at all in the last decade, then you already know. While people react differently to any given environment, and some people may experience more stress than others, certain aspects of the modern workplace tend to cause most people to experience stress.

- **Workload.** At one time, "multitasking" was not a commonly used word. Now it's a goal to which most of us aspire. People continually try to do more in less time and to get more done in a day. Much of the increase in workload is related to improved communication technologies and the resulting glut of incoming information that many experience at work. A survey of 1,200 workers of a variety of sorts found employees receiving an average of 200 messages a day when all media are included (i.e., e-mail, phone, memo, letter, etc.).[17] People are often faced with more work than they can complete during regular work hours. As many as 52 percent of North American workers put in more than 12 hours a day and 50 percent regularly skip lunch so they can complete their work.[18] Workload issues can be especially problematic for those who are not fitted well with their job and perhaps can't work as efficiently as others do or don't enjoy their work as much.

- **Social environment.** The social climate in the workplace can be a source of stress in many ways. In an environment that doesn't provide support for work-related issues or personal and family issues, a closed communication culture, a hostile environment, or an extremely competitive environment all can be stressful. Workplace romances that fail can also be a source of stress. More than half of human resource professionals report that workplace romances have had a negative impact on their organizations.[19]

- **Physical environment.** Aspects of the physical environment, such as loud noise, poor air circulation, or excessive heat can add to stress levels. An important recent development in offices in cities across the country is crowding. More employees are being squeezed into smaller spaces, often by creating cubicles from partitions that allow for little privacy. Sean Hutchinson, president of the New York–based Integra Realty Resources, Inc., calls it the "scrunch factor." According to Hutchinson, "The big guys take offices that are just as big or bigger than in the past, while the minions are getting stuffed into smaller and smaller spaces."[20] Social psychologists have long known that putting more people into smaller spaces can cause negative effects. In one study, researchers put ten people into an 8-by-12 foot room and ten people into a 20-by-30 foot room and then took some physical and psychological measurements. The people in the smaller room had higher blood pressure and heart rates than those in the larger room and made more errors on difficult mental tasks.[21]

- **Concerns over job.** Especially in tough economic times and in the industries most affected by them, people may experience concern over job security. Fear of downsizing can be distracting and stressful. In addition, eliminating jobs means those remaining must absorb more responsibilities, contributing to work overload. This stress can be reduced or alleviated to some degree by clear communication from management about the future and by allowing employees to participate in decision making to the extent possible.

Conflict Quote ▼

One of every eight workers works in a cubicle—and they show higher stress levels.

—Sean Hutchinson, President, Integra Realty Resources[22] ▲

POLICIES, PROCEDURES, AND NORMS

The written and unwritten rules in organizations can create a culture that encourages and even rewards conflict. A culture that creates excessive competition will create conflict as well. For example, organizations may have contests and prizes that encourage unnecessary competition and inhibit cooperation. Competition encourages employees to work harder for their own reward. It does not make them better employees, nor does it encourage them to have pride in their work. One survey of 1,200 employees at three different companies found that offering performance incentive pay actually de-motivated the majority of employees. In 1990, Rob Rodin ended the incentive programs at Marshall Industries, an electronics distributor based in El Monte, California. Over the next six years, employee turnover dropped by 85 percent, while sales grew from $565 million to $1.7 billion. "By paying well but knocking out pep rallies, contests, prizes, commissions, and individual bonuses, we became more collaborative and adaptable," says Rodin.[23]

In some organizations the procedures that employees are required to follow are not well thought out or have not changed with the changing needs of the organization and cause strife between employees. At one Midwestern plastics plant, maintenance technicians had the responsibility of maintaining and repairing three large blow-molding machines. When they needed parts, they wrote a note on a scrap of paper and handed it to the purchasing clerk. If the slips contained complete information, the clerk would type a purchase order and have it signed by the purchasing manager before the order could be placed. If the scrap of paper didn't include the necessary ordering information, the purchasing clerk had to wander around the production floor looking for a mechanic to get more details. When the clerk didn't have time for this, incomplete orders would be set aside. These cumbersome procedures made the process of getting a part annoyingly slow, so that when the items arrived, the impatient mechanics would take the parts from the dock before the receiving paperwork was completed. This procedure created problems later when the invoice for the part came in but purchasing would have no record of the part arriving.

> **Conflict Quote ▼**
>
> *The idea of merit rating is alluring, but the effect is exactly the opposite of what the words promise. Everyone propels himself forward, or tries to, for his own good, for his own life preserver. The organization is the loser.*
>
> —W. Edwards Deming[24] ▲

Several conflicts arose from these procedures. The purchasing clerk was often frustrated by orders with incomplete information and felt the mechanics were uncooperative. The mechanics were irritated with purchasing because it seemed to take so long to get parts. And accounting wasn't happy with purchasing because they had invoices they couldn't process.

The real problem wasn't any department or person but poorly considered procedures. An external consultant was hired to review the efficiency of the purchasing department and made significant improvements in the process of ordering repair and maintenance items. Mechanics were required to place orders by handwriting purchase orders, including part numbers, and placing the order in an inbox for purchasing. If the order was incomplete, it was returned to the mechanic via the mechanic's inbox. The receiving area was locked, so no items could be removed without being properly accounted for. The changes in procedures made the process more efficient and reduced the conflict.

Organizations often contribute to conflict among employees in other ways, as well. Unclear job descriptions and ambiguous lines of authority create confusion and frustration. Managers who transfer or promote difficult employees just to be rid of them simply spread dysfunction instead of rewarding worthy employees. Similarly, as equity theory suggests, managers who attempt to quiet complainers or troublemakers by giving them what they want can create a perception of social injustice among employees. Organizational policies or procedures can also create difficulties for people external to the organization, such as impersonal policies that prevent employees from satisfying customer needs or voice-mail systems that require callers to navigate their way through a maze of messages.

DIVERSITY

As we make achieving diversity a goal, we are often surprised by the challenges we encounter when we bring people with different ways of doing things together. Brian Lohr, Associate Director of Admissions for the MBA program at the University of Notre Dame, shared a story about a newly arrived Middle Eastern student. Brian's first meeting with the student had gone quite well—until the very end. As the meeting was finishing, Brian noticed a marked change in the student's demeanor. The student was visibly upset and Brian was confused. He asked the student if he had done something to offend him. The student replied that he had. As their meeting had come to an end, Brian had relaxed into his chair and crossed his legs, resting his ankle across his knee. In doing so he exposed the bottom of his shoe to the student, a profoundly offensive act in the student's native culture.

As we become a global economy, cultural diversity will become an increasingly critical factor in organizational success. Achieving diversity, however, is only part of the goal. While the recommendations in this book are based on conflicts in Western culture, the importance of learning how to work through conflict with people who are from diverse cultural backgrounds is undeniable. Culture refers to the shared values, beliefs, norms, language, and social institutions that guide everyday life for a group of people. Cultures vary in innumerable ways but a few major and important dimensions are worthy of your attention.

Cultures can be individualist or collectivist. This dimension reflects the degree to which individuals value their connection with the group versus their independence as individuals. Individualist cultures value independence over the group, whereas collectivist cultures place the group above the individual. The United States, Canada, and Western Europe are individualist cultures, while Asian and South American countries tend to be collectivist. Individualist and collectivist cultures approach conflict very differently. Collectivists often avoid conflict, preferring to maintain harmony and save

> **Conflict Quote ▼**
>
> *Diversity is not some vague, idealistic concept. The face of the workforce is changing, and, like it or not, here we come. Smart companies get it. Enlightened corporations know it's good for workers and good for the bottom line.*
>
> —Alexis Herman, United States Secretary of Labor, 1997–2001[25] ▲

"face." Individualists, on the other hand, don't enjoy conflict, certainly, but are much less likely to avoid it.[26]

Cultures also vary in communication styles. In some cultures, communication is very direct, while in others the style is indirect. In cultures featuring an indirect style, it is expected that relational exchanges will come before getting down to business. As a result, direct communication may be perceived as rude. Cultures with indirect styles of communication also tend to be highly context-dependent, wherein a great deal of the meaning of a message is derived from the context of the communication (who's in the room, what time of day we're meeting, where the exchange takes place, and so on). In some cultures, the style of communication is very expressive and animated, while in other cultures it is more reserved.[27]

Cultures may also differ in their interpretation of time. Some cultures value multitasking, while others prefer doing one thing at a time. Some cultures value punctuality, while others do not. These differences can become a problem when they are misinterpreted. An indirect style of communication can seem like disorganization to someone who is accustomed to a more direct, "get down to business" style. And a lack of concern for punctuality can be interpreted as a lack of consideration and professionalism. Learning about other cultures and managing expectations is crucial to preventing this type of misinterpretation.[28]

There are many ways to think about diversity in the workplace. Typically, when we refer to diversity we mean gender, racial, or ethnic diversity. But even people that look the same, share a common religion, and hail from the same place can hold very different attitudes, values, and beliefs. If you have siblings, then you know that even people who share some genetic material and have grown up in similar environments can vehemently disagree about a whole host of items. Dealing with differences can create stress and friction.

PSYCHOLOGICAL CONTEXT: RELATIONSHIP FACTORS

Any analysis should include an examination of the relationship between the parties. Communication between people creates a history that the people carry with them. The history, the patterns of communication, will shape expectations about future interactions and will influence how they turn out. Two aspects of the relationship are considered here: power and trust. Each has a profound effect on the communication of the parties and, therefore, their ability to effectively implement a communication approach to working through conflicts.

POWER

Power is about perceptions of control over others or the ability to influence others in some way. Power isn't something that is just "out there." It's a property of a relationship and results from the dependence of one person on another for the achievement of a goal. The amount of perceived power is affected by the importance of the goal and the alternatives for achieving the goal without depending on the powerful person.

Positions of power are created by people's needs and wants. If you have something that nobody wants, you don't have much power. But if you can help people get what they want or prevent them from getting what they want, you are in a powerful position. A now-classic way to think about power identifies five sources of power: legitimate power, reward power, coercive power, expert power, and referent power. **Legitimate power** comes from the authority assigned to a position that a person holds. Managers and supervisors have legitimate power over their direct reports. But people in organizations also develop power through resources, relationships, and expertise. If you have control over the distribution or withholding of valuable resources, you have **reward power** and can influence the behavior of those who depend on you for those resources. Conversely, if you have the ability to punish others in some way and can control them, you have **coercive power.** If you have valuable information, know the answers, or can solve a problem, you have some measure of **expert power.** If you are well liked and people want to be liked by you, or if you have qualities that are socially appealing such as good persuasive speaking skills, you have a certain amount of influence over others through **referent power.** Typically, people develop some sources of power in their organization but not all.[29]

When conflicts develop, the power distribution in a relationship suddenly becomes more important. But who has which power in a conflict is not always clear. Conflict makes people emotional, and when emotions are high, people often feel helpless and may underestimate just how much power they have. In their book on interpersonal conflict, William Wilmot and Joyce Hocker offer this rule of thumb: Each party in a conflict will always believe that the other party has more power.[30]

Managers dealing with conflict should carefully analyze the power structures of the conflicting parties. Sometimes this is difficult because not only do the conflicting parties have low levels of confidence in their own power, but also communication between conflicting parties may not always reveal the true power dynamics. People can talk about what they did or what they decided without necessarily mentioning the people who influenced them. For example, Juan may be upset with Jennifer for not supporting an idea in a meeting. When asked to explain, Jennifer may not say that the referent power of LaToya, who also failed to support the idea, was an influencing factor, but may instead simply cite some problems with the idea.[31]

Sometimes power issues are themselves at the root of a conflict. People may feel that others are trying to gain power over them, which they choose to reject. Comments such as these reveal this sort of thinking:

- You're just trying to control me.
- You can't tell me what to do.
- You're not my boss.
- Who do you think you are?
- What makes you think you have the right to. . . ?

Power affects the choices people make when they respond to conflict. In situations in which conflict occurs between parties with higher and lower levels of power, the party with lower power may feel that the options available are limited. Formal grievance procedures offer employees an opportunity to be heard in these situations. In the absence of this alternative, or if this alternative has proven ineffective in the past, employees may resort to withholding information, complaining to others, calling in sick, making mistakes, and other indirect responses. As Wilmot and Hocker point out, power corrupts, but so does powerlessness.[32]

In addition to ensuring that an effective grievance process is in place, what can managers do to help employees deal with this type of situation more effectively? The main goal is to balance the perception of power somewhat. Empowering employees is an effort to achieve that sense of balance and increase employees' feelings of control. Organizations empower their employees in a number of ways. Organizational hierarchies can be flattened; managers can use a more participative leadership style; and impersonalized forms of power, such as rules or regulations, can be put in place, reducing the perceived personalized power of those with higher levels of power.[33]

Conflicts between higher- and lower-status employees may be especially common during times of change. A good manager creates and guides change and also considers how changes in the organization will affect employees, not just in the tasks they perform but also how they feel. Managers can empower their employees during times of change by letting them participate in the process and by emphasizing a "we" approach in the organization. Employees who feel that their needs have been considered will also feel that they are valued as employees and will be more supportive of change.

People with lower levels of power can affect the outcomes of conflicts with people who have more power, despite their obvious disadvantage. Those with more power might be willing to restrain themselves from using it if they recognize the benefits of doing so. Parties with lower levels of power can make progress in these conflicts by being persistent, without being overly emotional. They can point out the advantages to the high-power party of coming to an agreement, and they can attempt to address the difficulties those with more power anticipate if the goals of those with less power are met.[34]

Conflict in organizations is not limited to parties of unequal power. Parties of equal power may have interdependency through shared resources or reliance on each other to complete tasks. When in conflict, these parties often engage in win/lose bargaining strategies that escalate conflict rather than resolve it and negatively affect the functioning of the organization. The conflicting parties may be unable to clearly communicate with each other. Task-interdependent departments may fail to coordinate their efforts effectively and may argue over who is supposed to do what. One party may attempt to strengthen its position in the organization by denigrating others, and those who share important resources may begin to demand their own.[36]

Conflict Quote ▼

As a general rule, it makes sense to use power only as a last resort. When you use power you win and the other loses. More often than not, resentment and alienation accompany this action.
—John Ford, Mediation Training Institute[35] ▲

Managers can help in this situation by clearly assigning roles, promoting a culture of teamwork, and attaching efforts to outcomes. They can reduce interdependency between parties or, alternatively, increase it to the point where parties can't risk the conflict. They may take measures to strengthen the relationships within the organization and to improve the attitudes employees have toward the organization. Of course, even with these efforts, conflicts will occur. To be ready for them, organizations can train employees to communicate effectively and to negotiate so they can manage most conflicts on their own. For more serious conflicts, managers can establish a central figure to regulate or arbitrate conflicts in order to protect the organization from business problems.[37]

Middle managers may find themselves caught between higher-powered and lower-powered parties in conflict, which can be a source of intrapersonal conflict for managers who feel obligations to both of these groups. Middle managers may prefer simply to stay out of it, but that can be a difficult position to maintain, especially if the two parties keep trying to pull the manager into the conflict. Other options for middle managers include choosing one group to side with, trying to satisfy both sides, or stalling and hoping the parties work things out.[38]

TRUST

In organizations, trust occurs at different levels. At the organizational level, trust occurs within the organizational system and between the system and the environment. Unethical practices in an organization have a devastating effect on trust, both internal and external to the organization. WorldCom and Enron are well-known examples of organizations that lost trust at a macrolevel through unethical actions.

Within the organization, trust, or the lack of it, is part of an organization's culture. The structure of an organization, its written policies, and unspoken norms work to create and communicate the presence or absence of trust. Flatter structures and employee empowerment communicate the organization's trust in its employees and can, in turn, engender employee trust in the organization. The words and actions of individual managers can also engender trust. Managers who say what they mean and do what they say they will are trusted.

Trust in organizations can take a variety of forms.[39]

- **Trust in ability.** For managers and employees alike, it's important to trust in the ability of others to do their job. Micromanaging is an expression of lack of trust in employees.
- **Trust in a commitment to the relationship.** Managers want to know that employees are going to stay with the organization, and employees want to feel that their jobs are secure. In difficult economic times, when downsizing is a popular survival strategy for organizations, trust in relational commitment suffers.
- **Trust in the other's concern for your welfare.** At work and in other areas of our lives, we are suspicious of people who do not seem to have our best interest at heart.
- **Trust in another's regard for privileged information.** In organizations, managers and employees must be able to trust that disclosed confidential information will not be shared with others or be used against the discloser.

The existence of trust is important for working through conflicts constructively because it affects the process in several ways. Working through conflicts collaboratively requires sharing information. Parties must be willing to share their interests and goals with each other in order to discover what really matters. But as we just saw, information can be a source of power. Parties must trust that the information they share will not be used against them in some way. They must believe that the others at the table will work for a mutually satisfying solution to a problem and not resort to using force or threats to get the best solution for themselves. Trust must be present for conflicting parties to communicate openly with each other about their interests.

Trust and open communication are also required for building relationships through collaborative processes. However, relationship building may not always be required or even desired in every conflict situation. The simplicity of the parties' goals and the degree and duration of interdependency may make it more or less desirable to develop the relationship. For example, parties in conflict over a single transaction are interdependent but only until the transaction is completed and so may not be concerned with real relationship building. In that case, they could reach a useful agreement without really trusting each other.

When relationships are important, parties can build trust by being courteous, sincere, fair, and not losing control. Over time, trust develops when all parties are honest, reliable, and competent.[41] Other behaviors that promote trust include appropriate self-disclosure. Revealing small amounts of appropriate information communicates trust. When this disclosure is reciprocated and repeated, trust grows. Communication behaviors that demonstrate acceptance, such as listening attentively, asking questions to clarify understanding, and giving affirming feedback also help build trust.[42]

INDIVIDUAL FACTORS

CONFLICT MANAGEMENT STYLES

No discussion of conflict management would be complete without discussing styles of conflict management. Conflict management style refers to the preferred way an individual responds to conflict. Most style theorists do not suggest that a person responds to all conflict in a certain way, but rather that people have a preferred way of responding that they will use if factors do not influence them to use another style.

Numerous typologies have been proposed to classify ways of responding, from a dichotomy of cooperation and competition to more recent complex two-dimensional grids that produce five styles (see Table 2-2). Two of these models seem to be most popular. In one, the dimensions of the grid represent the *degree of concern* for self and the degree of concern for others when responding to conflict. In the other, the dimensions represent *levels of cooperation* and *levels of aggressiveness*. Both models produce a similar collection of five styles: avoiding, obliging or accommodating, dominating or competing, integrating or collaborating, and compromising.[43]

Table 2-2   Conflict Management Styles

Conflict management styles result from the combination of the degree of concern an individual has for one's self, or aggressiveness, and the degree of concern an individual has for the other, or cooperation, when responding to conflict.

Concern for Self, Aggressiveness	Concern for Others, Cooperation	Conflict Handling, Style
Low	Low	Avoiding
Low	High	Obliging or Accommodating
High	Low	Dominating or Competing
High	High	Integrating or Collaborating
Moderate	Moderate	Compromising

An **avoiding style** is characterized by a desire to avoid confrontation, disagreements, and unpleasant exchanges with others. There are times when, due to situational factors, each of us might decide that we are better off not expressing conflict. Perhaps the issue is not important enough to us (I'd rather have Italian for lunch, but you want Mexican), or perhaps the relationship is not very important, desirable, or enduring (the temporary receptionist keeps mispronouncing your name). In some cases, the costs of confrontation can be too high, for example, if an issue is raised with a superior in the organization who may respond negatively. At times, we may avoid conflict for the benefit of the other party. (This person can't handle this information right now.) But when people prefer to avoid conflict regardless of situational factors, and they use various strategies to maintain avoidance, they are demonstrating an avoiding style of conflict management.[44]

You can avoid conflict in a number of ways. A common technique is withdrawal or refusal to participate in the conflict. Avoidance can also be achieved by denying that a problem exists or claiming that resolution of the conflict is hopeless, so participating in the conflict is pointless. Intimidating someone else so that an issue is never raised is another time-tested way to avoid a conflict.

When people employ an avoidant style, conflicts can escalate because they aren't being resolved or managed. The other party may be unaware of the nature of the conflict because it hasn't been expressed directly, so members of the party may unwittingly engage in behaviors that exacerbate the problem. When the other party *is* aware of the problem, failure to raise an issue may be perceived as a lack of concern or interest. Although the avoiding parties are unlikely to directly express the conflict to the other party, they are likely to talk about it to others in the organization. This, too, can lead to escalation as the parties being avoided may discover they are being talked about "behind their backs."[45]

Avoiding conflict can lead to more avoidance. Because of the tendency for avoidance to escalate conflict, conflicts that have been avoided may eventually grow to the point where they simply must be confronted. Often this need for confrontation occurs after negative emotions have festered, our worst thoughts about the other party have been confirmed, and many third parties have been made aware of the situation. At this point, it may be even more difficult for parties to handle the confrontation well, which can end up confirming the negative expectations about conflict that kept the avoiding person from raising the issue in the first place and can ultimately lead to more avoidance.[46]

The **obliging** or **accommodating style** is characterized by a preference for cooperation, a willingness to make concessions, and by giving in to the wishes of others. The accommodating style puts harmony between parties ahead of individual needs and interests, which is a useful strategy in some situations, such as when an issue is very important to one person but not to the other. In certain situations we all accommodate or oblige. For example, we may feel that the other party in a conflict has more power and that accommodation is the only alternative.[47]

Sometimes when people accommodate, they say "yes" when they would rather say "no" because they feel the need to be compassionate or to avoid hurting someone. However, people who frequently give in for the good of others may accommodate or oblige resentfully. They may become complainers, play the martyr, or give in when there is no compelling reason, simply to demonstrate how nice they are.[48]

Accommodators often don't recognize that it is possible to refuse someone compassionately. People who have a difficult time saying no often don't place as much importance on their own feelings as they do on the feelings of others. But they can learn communication skills that allow them to express an understanding of the other person's feelings without ignoring their own, thus making it easier for them to stand their ground. They often need to learn that it's okay to have boundaries and limits.[49]

In contrast to the agreeableness of the accommodating style, the **dominating** or **competing style** of conflict management is confrontational and characterized by a win/lose mindset. Those who use this style like to argue their position but, if that isn't working, will use their power or authority to get their way. Individuals who prefer this style are more interested in winning the conflict than in reaching a solution that satisfies both parties. In fact, for some the "win" must be at the expense of the other party to be truly satisfying. This lack of concern for the other party is evident in this style by a tendency toward put-downs and personal attacks. This style can often lead to destructive conflict as parties engage in an exchange of insults, verbal abuse, and threats.[50]

However, the dominating or competing style isn't always destructive, and, in some cases, it may be the most appropriate style. A person's role may require a dominating or competing style. In a courtroom, for example, lawyers compete. In organizations, managers are sometimes required to make decisions and give directions that will not be well received but are unavoidable, such as when an organization is downsizing.[51]

The **integrating** or **collaborating style** is most effective when the option to negotiate for a mutually satisfying outcome exists. This style seeks creative and innovative win/win solutions to problems. In addition, the collaborative processes themselves can build relationships. This style clearly demands more energy and time than the others, so it may not always be the best choice. It is the appropriate strategy when both parties care about the goals and the relationship.[52]

Successful collaboration is accomplished through communication. Collaborative communication tools help parties understand each other's perspective, making it possible for both parties to work toward creating mutually satisfying solutions. We'll look more closely at collaborative communication techniques in Chapter 3.

The **compromising style** seeks the middle ground. Each party gives a little and gets a little. Sometimes compromising is the best strategy. For example, a compromise can yield fair results with little time invested when an issue is not terribly important. But compromising means that no one gets exactly what he or she wants. So compromising doesn't necessarily result in parties who are satisfied with the results of the resolution. Each party may have to give up something important. Compromise is often a default strategy that circumvents true problem solving and doesn't allow parties to realize the benefits of conflict.[53]

Though people may have a preference for one style of response to conflict, they can and do use different styles in different situations. For example, in organizational settings, employees are more likely to be accommodating or obliging with the boss. Recent research shows that, rather than relying solely on one style for a given conflict, people typically use a pattern of styles. They may strategically switch styles as they notice the one they are using isn't working.[54]

Despite our ability to use many styles, we may tend habitually to overuse one conflict management style across many diverse situations, whether that style is most appropriate or not. Managers can make the most out of learning about conflict management styles by recognizing which styles are most effective in different situations and by making sure they and their employees are competent in using each of the styles. Being flexible in the style used is crucial to successful management and resolution of conflict. Examples of situations in which each of these styles is most appropriate are given in Table 2-3. Note that some of these situations could be moments in an ongoing conflict; the style choice for that moment would represent one style used in a pattern of styles.[55]

Table 2-3   Communication Indicators and Various Situations in which a Particular Conflict Management Style may be Appropriate

Style	Situations in Which Each Style Is Appropriate	Communication Indicators of Style
Avoiding	<ul><li>The issue is unimportant.</li><li>The relationship is unimportant.</li><li>One or both of the parties needs a "time-out" from the conflict.</li><li>The risk of confronting outweighs the potential benefits significantly.</li></ul>	Avoiding communication seeks to deny or dismiss the conflict, make a joke of it, or change the subject.<ul><li>I don't want to talk about it.</li><li>Everyone gets in a bad mood occasionally.</li><li>How 'bout them Cubs?</li></ul>
Obliging or Accommodating	<ul><li>A requirement for competition is part of your role.</li><li>You are making an unpopular decision from a position of authority.</li><li>Others do not have the resources to make a good decision.</li></ul>	Obliging or accommodating communication yields to the other party.<ul><li>It's up to you. Whatever you want is fine with me.</li><li>I don't care.</li></ul>
Dominating or Competing	<ul><li>Time is available.</li><li>The issue is important.</li><li>The relationship is important.</li><li>Parties are willing and able to participate in problem solving.</li><li>Having all parties involved will improve the quality of the solution.</li></ul>	Dominating or competing seeks to persuade or force the other party to change positions and to control the other party.<ul><li>You're being ridiculous.</li><li>Oh yeah, that's a really *great* [sarcastically] idea.</li><li>That's your responsibility, not mine.</li></ul>
Integrating or Collaborating	<ul><li>Time is available.</li><li>The issue is important.</li><li>The relationship is important.</li><li>Parties are willing and able to participate in problem solving.</li><li>Having all parties involved will improve the quality of the solution.</li></ul>	Integrating or collaborating focuses on reaching an understanding of the different parties' perspectives and working toward a solution that satisfies each party's interests.<ul><li>"When you said that, did you mean. . . ?"</li><li>"I can see how that would be upsetting to you."</li><li>"I can do more of that."</li></ul>
Compromising	<ul><li>Other styles have been tried and failed.</li><li>Quick, temporary solution is needed.</li><li>Parties are equally powerful and goals are mutually exclusive.</li></ul>	Compromising communication attempts to work out a fair solution.<ul><li>If you're willing to do without this, I'll be willing to do without that.</li><li>I'll do this today, if you do it tomorrow.</li></ul>

Conflict management style is a product of the parties' communication. Attending to communication can reveal to parties and observers what styles the parties are using. It is important to note that style does not result simply from the intention to use a particular style. For example, a party may intend to be integrating but may be perceived as competing due to ineffective communication.[56] Table 2-3 provides examples of communication indicators of the different styles.

PERSONALITY

Many conflicts are rooted in **personality** clashes. Different personalities produce different ideas about what and how things should be done. This very diversity is what many organizations strive to achieve in their workforce so they can benefit from decision making and problem solving done with varied perspectives and expertise. Research on teamwork suggests that diverse teams do produce better solutions to complex problems, but it takes them a little bit longer to get there. Most organizations seem to believe the benefits are worth the extra effort.

Understanding the nature of personality can help managers and employees view individual differences in a more positive way. People think about personality in terms of types and traits. **Traits** are enduring characteristics that individuals display, and **personality types** are categories of personalities that share a collection of traits. People with different personality types, who share few common traits, may have difficulty seeing eye-to-eye. This difficulty can lead to destructive conflict if we make negative inferences about the other's behaviors. Consider the situation of Li and Brad, two very different personalities who were members of an MBA team working to prepare a marketing plan for a new business. At the very first team meeting, Li produced a timeline for the creation of the marketing plan. He had divided the project into smaller tasks, arranged them in sequence, and assigned a deadline for each task. At the next team meeting, he distributed the timeline and wanted to assign members of the team to the different tasks. Li saw this as a way to help the team get off to a good start, but Brad didn't share that view. He saw the timeline as premature and restricting. Brad felt that some tasks would require more research than others, and he wanted to have plenty of time to explore any relevant information. Furthermore, he thought Li was acting overly controlling and that preparing a timeline without input from the rest of the team was inappropriate.

Clashes of personality such as this one can lead to personal attacks and quickly spiral out of control. But diversity among personalities doesn't have to result in destructive conflict if people can learn to value differences and recognize how they contribute to better outcomes. In the preceding example, the team valued working together and learned how to appreciate the contributions that each member made. In the end, Brad recognized that Li's schedule helped keep them on track, and Li remained flexible enough to skip a task in the sequence on his timeline because more information was desired.

Still, we've all encountered what we would call "difficult people." Were those experiences just the result of our inability to tolerate diversity or our lack of effective communication skills? Probably neither. Research shows that there are, indeed, some personalities that are more prone to destructive conflict than others. For example, people who are highly authoritarian have a tendency to judge others by a rigid set of moral standards; to identify with high-status individuals; and to reject, criticize, and punish low-status individuals. Closely related is dogmatism. Dogmatic individuals are close-minded and inflexible, with very little tolerance for other points of view. Individuals high in either of these characteristics can be difficult to work with and for.[57]

Individuals high in codependence can also create challenges for workplace relations. Codependent individuals have difficulty keeping a healthy psychological distance between themselves and others. They feel the need to control the behavior of others and are not able to detach themselves appropriately from the consequences of the behaviors of others. Codependent people usually have low levels of trust. They tend to hoard information as something to be controlled. They also operate from the mindset that there are never enough resources to go around. They hide their feelings and let them simmer under the façade of feeling what is expected of them, and they may experience low self-esteem or be terribly upset when things change. Such people tend to take things very personally and have difficulty separating accountability from blame. As you can well imagine, these people can be difficult to work with, and the combination of behavioral tendencies associated with codependence is particularly unfortunate for effective conflict management. Not only do codependent individuals fail to communicate openly, it is difficult for others to communicate openly with them because they are so easily offended.[58]

Conflict Quote ▼

An employee with an attitude problem is a manager's nightmare. When the problem is an entitlement mentality—evidenced by rolling eyeballs, sighs, and antagonistic body language—it can drive managers crazy because stopping such "silent" behavior is difficult when employees so easily can deny there's a problem.
—Paul Facone, Director of Employment and Development, Paramount Pictures[59] ▲

MESSAGES AND FEEDBACK: WHEN COMMUNICATION MAKES IT WORSE

This book posits the idea that the most effective way to work through conflict is by engaging conflicting parties in the communication process. But conflicts are not simply resolved through communication. They are initiated, maintained, and escalated through communication, as well. Managers can use the messages exchanged between parties to diagnose whether a conflict is constructive or destructive. If the messages reveal a task-oriented, cognitive conflict, a manager may wisely decide to let it be. However, if conflict messages contain ego attacks and abusive language, action on the part of the manager may be required.

Abusive language, or verbal aggression, uses words to injure another person's self-concept. This aggression may include insults, character judgments, and hurtful comments, such as "You're an idiot" or "Why don't you do us all a favor and quit?" Abusive language tends to be vague ("You're such a loser") and ineffective at creating change. Yet some people when confronted with conflict immediately resort to the strategy of attacking another person's character. Some who frequently use this strategy think many of their comments are genuinely humorous. Others, however, don't see them that way and find verbal aggressors less credible and without as many legitimate arguments as those who refrain from verbal aggression. Furthermore, in the workplace, if a higher-status person ridicules a lower-status person's mode of speech or clothing, or negatively labels him or her (e.g., whiner, screw-up), it may be considered harassment.[60]

Look at the following examples of verbal aggression:

- You are completely incompetent.
- Did you dress with the lights off this morning?

- You talk like a first-grader.
- You have absolutely no class.

Other communication techniques that can escalate a conflict, or at the minimum stall any chance of resolution, include:[61]

- **Mindreading.** In a conflict, we often think we know more than we really do about the other party and why they've done what they have done. We may *tell* them why they did something or what they were thinking, rather than asking them. And the motives and thoughts we imagine to be true are typically negative.
- **Self-summarizing.** When people self-summarize, they keep repeating what they have already said. They communicate no new information, but what's worse is that they ignore the responses of the other party.
- **Cross-complaining.** When parties cross-complain, they each are sharing complaints and no one is listening. "You've been late to our team meetings three times this week." "And *you've* forgotten to post the minutes to the web site."
- **Kitchen-sinking.** Conflicts can escalate when the parties bring up more and more issues and throw "everything but the kitchen sink" into the conflict.

Of course, not all communication comes from words. In fact, some anthropologists think that only about 7 percent of the meaning of a message is derived from the verbal content.[62] The rest is nonverbal. Nonverbal communication is important in all of our face-to-face interactions, but it's a critical aspect of conflict communication. Nonverbal communication is vitally important to the communication of our attitudes and emotions and in helping others know how to interpret our verbal message. The same words accompanied by a smile have a very different meaning when yelled and accompanied by a clenched fist.

The meaning of most nonverbal cues is culture-based, but certain facial expressions (anger is one of them) are recognized across cultures. In Western culture, we communicate an interest in what someone else is saying through making eye contact, leaning toward the person, and showing facial expressions. We can just as easily communicate that we don't agree with another person and even that we don't value or respect that person through our nonverbal communication. A listener who rolls her eyes, crosses her arms, looks away, slouches down in her seat, shakes her head "no" continually, and wears a rejecting scowl on her face is communicating more than "I don't agree with the point you're making." She's also communicating that "I don't care about the point you're making *and* I don't care about you." These nonverbal messages can make collaborative communication between parties all but impossible and can be so frustrating that they actually escalate conflict.

LEVEL OF CONFLICT AS A FACTOR IN THE SYSTEM

At the beginning of this chapter, we discussed the different social levels at which conflict can occur. At each level of conflict, factors unique to that level can contribute to the conflict and should be considered in your analysis.

INTRAPERSONAL FACTORS

A specific form of intrapersonal conflict frequently experienced in the workplace is known as role conflict. A *role* is the collection of behaviors and attitudes commonly expected from someone who occupies a particular social position.[63] For example, a receptionist has a social role. We expect a receptionist to be friendly, efficient, and have good phone manners. Teacher, CEO, administrative assistant, mother, and priest are all examples of social roles. Each of us occupies numerous social roles and, as a result, can experience role conflict. A role **conflict** occurs when the expectations for one role clash with the expectations for another.[64] For example, a commonly experienced form of role conflict occurs when people seek to balance work and family life. A working parent with a sick child may experience role conflict because the expectation for the parent role would be to stay home and care for the sick child, but the expectation for the employee role would be to go to work. Many organizations understand this sort of role conflict and create policies to assist their employees to manage it; such policies can greatly reduce the amount of stress and internal conflict experienced by literally everyone in the organization.

Managers also can help employees avoid experiencing intrapersonal conflict by periodically assessing employee-job fit. Employees can experience intrapersonal conflict if they are asked to perform tasks for which they are not adequately prepared, or if they are expected to do more than they can accomplish. Furthermore, they can experience conflict if their own goals are at odds with the goals of their department or organization. Some organizations actually encourage intrapersonal conflict through conflicting goals and policies and unclear expectations.[65]

INTERPERSONAL FACTORS

Interpersonal conflicts are quite common in organizations and can be particularly perplexing for mid-level managers.[66] For conflicts that occur at the interpersonal level, the nature of the relationship between the parties is the most important factor to analyze. In organizations, as was previously noted, differences in status will have an effect on how conflicts are likely to be expressed. But interpersonal relationships are defined by much more than positions in an organizational hierarchy.

Interpersonal conflicts are often influenced by a strong relationship history. These can be difficult to analyze from the outside. A remark or behavior that seems perfectly innocent to an outsider may be laden with meaning to the conflicting parties. Part of the relationship history can include patterns that are associated with recurring conflict. Patterns may emerge in the way that the conflict begins, the response of the parties, and the outcomes. Analyzing these patterns can be the first step in preventing the conflict from reoccurring.

Consider, if you will, an administrative assistant who has been in the same position for several years. Because the office has been reorganized, she no longer works for the person who hired her but now has several bosses and frequently finds herself in conflict with one in particular. The new boss tends to overcommit himself, get behind in his work, and then demand that the assistant invest extra time in getting her projects done at the expense of her other bosses or personal time. When the boss takes on another project, the assistant knows what's coming, but she never raises the issue because she feels that, since the reorganization, her job may be in jeopardy. Instead, she becomes unpleasant and complains to anyone who will listen. After a while, the pattern is familiar and frustrating to her and really annoying to those who must listen to her complaints.

After a while, this sort of microevent can be fairly easy to recognize. Even the parties involved know the pattern but may be unable to see how they are contributing to its continuance. Managers investigating these conflicts can begin by asking questions about how they are initiated, who responds and how, and what would happen if the conflict went away. They may explore the possibility that the conflict serves some function for the system.[67]

INTERGROUP FACTORS

Intergroup conflict is possible anytime there are two or more clearly delineated groups in an organization. The groups we are part of are called **ingroups,** and the groups to which we do not belong are called **outgroups.** We develop part of our identity from our group memberships. We are democrats, we are Catholics, we are Americans, and we are parents. All of these memberships mean something to us and contribute to our identity. Similarly, in organizations, we gain part of our identity from the groups we claim as ours. We are part of the marketing department. We are the plastics division. We are plant 16. We are the first shift.

Because we derive part of our identity from our social groups, we are motivated to see those groups in a positive light. In fact, we are motivated to view them more positively than other groups. After all, if another group was better than our own, wouldn't we be a member of that group instead? Favoring your own group is called *ingroup bias*. Research shows that even when people know that they are part of a group that has been created by randomly assigning group membership to one of two groups, they believe the group they are part of is better than the other group.[68]

Not only do people show this almost automatic favoritism toward their own groups, they can be equally motivated to show outgroups unfavorably. People often contribute to the positive perception of their own group by denigrating outgroups. They tend to show more cooperation with their ingroup and more competition with the outgroup. In addition, people tend to view their ingroup as being heterogeneous, while viewing the outgroup as being "all alike."[69]

Conflict Quote ▼

We define [diversity] as any collective mixture characterized by differences and similarities. That definition takes into consideration race and gender, plus behavioral diversity. A lot of times, you think you have diversity representation because a lot of individuals in a room look different, or they may have different educational experiences, geographic locations, or differences of origin. But, if you have invited all of these people into the room expecting them to assimilate into the environment, then you have diversity representation without true diversity.

    —Melanie L. Harrington, Executive Director, American Institute
      for Managing Diversity, Inc.[70] ▲

Once people develop a negative perception about an outgroup, the perception can be difficult to change. When people believe something about a social group, they tend to be more attentive to behaviors from group members that confirm their belief and less attentive to disconfirming behaviors. Similarly, people tend to jump to conclusions about correlations between something observed in one member of a group and the group as a whole. For example, let's say that in your organization your ingroup is "nonsmokers" and the outgroup is "smokers." You observe someone you know to be a smoker throwing a candy wrapper on the floor in the breakroom. Furthermore, you notice that outside around the company picnic table where some people eat their lunch in the summer, there are numerous cigarette butts. You may conclude that smokers are slobs. The fact may be that one or two smokers litter and the rest don't. And it may be that an equal percentage of nonsmokers also litter. But because of ingroup bias, you are more likely to notice the littering of a smoker and more likely to believe that all smokers are litterbugs. The habit of littering then becomes another point of differentiation between your group and the outgroup, making a positive attitude toward the outgroup even less likely to develop.

A negative attitude toward a group or members of a group because of their group membership is a form of prejudice. Prejudice (or *judging before knowing*) is associated with beliefs about a social group that contribute to the negative evaluation of its members. The collection of beliefs we hold about a social group is called a stereotype. Stereotyping, you may recall, is attributing to all members of a group or class those characteristics or behaviors observed in just one or a few. Although we tend to think of stereotypes as negative ("Overweight people are lazy"), they can be positive as well ("Overweight people are jolly"). But all stereotypes generalize beliefs across a social group and are commonly used to make hasty, often negative, judgments about members of an outgroup.

A popular example of intergroup conflict in organizations is the line and staff conflict. In an organization, the line generally refers to the production department, although in a nonmanufacturing facility, the customer service–oriented workers could be considered the line. The staff refers to the nonmanagement employees who support the line, such as human resources or quality control. These groups often have different goals within the organization. Line workers generally focus on aspects of the daily operations of the organization while staff workers may have more long-range goals. These groups also frequently have different backgrounds and values.[71]

Organizations can contribute to conflict between line and staff by enhancing the perception of status differences through matters of distributive justice. For instance, one organization created three separate classes of employees: management, clerical, and production. Management employees were salaried, while clerical and production workers were paid hourly. Although their hourly wages were similar, the clerical and production employees were very distinct groups with an undercurrent of conflict between them. In part, this conflict resulted from issues of distributive justice. In some cases, what might be perceived as an unfair distribution of rewards simply couldn't be avoided. For example, the production area was hot, noisy, and smelled like chemicals, while the staff offices were climate-controlled and quiet. The nature of their various jobs made these differences unavoidable. However, the organization contributed to the feelings of division between the groups in other ways. For example, production employees ate lunch in a break-room, while clerical employees were permitted to eat in a conference room. Production employees had to punch the clock, while clerical employees were permitted to handwrite their time cards.

Just as organizations can help create conflict between groups, they can help prevent it as well. Establishing superordinate goals is one way to foster cooperation in place of competition. A **superordinate goal** is one that cannot be achieved without the participation of both groups. In order to be effective, the goal must be one that both groups will benefit from achieving. In a now-famous study, Muzafer Sherif looked first at the effects of competition over scarce resources and then at the effects of superordinate goals on two groups of 11-year-old boys. Twenty-two boys from Oklahoma City were invited to a Boy Scouts of America camp that was surrounded by Robbers Cave State Park. The groups of boys arrived in two different buses on different days and for a while were unaware of each other's presence. The groups had their own cabins, and though they shared a mess hall, swimming area, recreation room, and athletic field, their movements through the campground were carefully orchestrated so they would not cross paths. That is, until one day when one of the groups, the Rattlers, overheard the other group, the

Eagles, playing on the athletic field as they walked through the woods nearby. After the groups became aware of each other, they expressed an interest in playing each other in a game of base-ball. The researchers, to create competition over scarce resources, planned a tournament of various games and contests with prizes for the winning group. During the period of competition, the groups began name-calling, teasing, making up derogatory songs, and raiding each other's cabins. After a while, the groups couldn't stand each other.

At that point, the researchers began their strategy for reducing the friction between the groups. The competitions were ended and contact between the groups was arranged for various tasks. However, mere contact was not enough to reduce the friction. The researchers introduced a number of superordinate goals, such as moving large boulders to "fix a problem" with the camp's water system, pooling the groups' money to pay for a film both groups wanted to see, pulling a stalled truck with a rope, and so on. After engaging in these activities and achieving several of their superordinate goals, the groups were civil, even friendly, with each other.[72]

What else can organizations do to minimize intergroup conflict?

- **Create a superordinate category.** A superordinate category is a larger category that subsumes the smaller social groups in the organization. Creating a culture in which employees perceive different groups as part of an organization-wide group or team with everyone sharing common goals can reduce intergroup conflict.
- **Flatten organizational structures in order to reduce status differences.** Although flatter hierarchies can lead to less formal communication and perhaps incivility, the tensions that naturally occur as a result of clearly delineated groups and status differences will be curtailed.
- **Decrease the competition over scarce resources.** Make sure that groups have the resources they need. Scarce resources should be distributed in ways that de-emphasize competition between groups.
- **Use "we" statements.** Using "we" statements instead of "I" statements, and "us" statements instead of "me" statements, communicates a larger, single category.

INTRAGROUP FACTORS

The complete absence of all conflict within a group is not a desirable state. The tendency for people in a group to always agree, conform to the group, and avoid openly dissenting (even though they may be dissenting privately) is sometimes called "groupthink" and can lead to tragic outcomes. After the space shuttle *Challenger* disintegrated before horrified onlookers only moments after its launch, President Reagan appointed a commission to investigate the cause of the accident. The cause was determined to be rocket fuel spewing from a joint that was supposed to be sealed by a failed rubber O-ring. It was also revealed that there had been some concern about the O-rings before the launch. The day before the launch, engineers from the group that manufactured the rocket's motor expressed concerns that the flight might be risky because the O-rings had never been tested below 53 degrees and the morning of the launch was expected to be in the low 20s. They feared the cold would affect the O-rings' resiliency and ability to seal the joint and said the flight should be a "no-go." But NASA launch personnel discounted their concerns and encouraged them to rethink their "no-go" recommendation. After a private meeting with the company's executives, the engineers changed their decision to "A-OK." Jesse Moore, Associate Administrator for Space Flight at NASA Headquarters was at the top of the launch decision chain. He had the power to approve or scrub the shuttle mission. He was advised that the *Challenger* was flight-ready and was told nothing about the concern with the O-rings. He had every reason to believe that everything was "A-OK" at the time of the launch.[73]

Groupthink can happen in highly cohesive groups that discourage dissent within the group and are insulated from other sources of dissenting information. In the *Challenger* example, the engineers were pressured into changing their recommendation and keeping their concerns to themselves. Jesse Moore was shielded by his advisors from the argument for postponing the launch.

Cohesiveness refers to the feelings of attraction the members of the group have for the group. For members of highly cohesive groups, membership is desirable and important. High cohesion does not automatically mean that a group will suffer from the disastrous decision making associated with groupthink. That sort of problem occurs when maintaining the chummy atmosphere of the group takes priority over making good decisions. In general, group cohesion is desirable and is positively related to levels of cognitive conflict and, as might be expected, negatively related to affective conflict.[75]

Groups develop their own implicit and explicit rules and expectations for behavior. Patterns of communication develop that define relationships within the group. Some members of the group will be closer to each other than other members and will form coalitions. Those who are coalesced will communicate with each other more, share more information, and feel closer to each other. Coalitions tend to form for a reason. Those who are closer may have more in common or give each other support. More than one coalition may form, but not everyone in the group will necessarily be included in any coalitions. Isolates, or those excluded from the coalition, may feel left out and rationalize their exclusion by asserting their disinterest in becoming part of a coalition. Among those who are in the coalition, an ingroup bias can develop, with the rest of the group viewed as an outgroup.[76]

Managers can analyze the relationships within a group by looking at the behaviors and patterns of communication among the group members. Particularly important in conflict situations are patterns of behavior that are repeated and lead to the same undesirable outcome. As with interpersonal relationships, toxic patterns of interaction occasionally develop in groups; however, group members may be too tightly connected as a system to recognize the problem and correct it themselves. Managers can learn about these patterns by observing the behavior of group members and, more directly, through interviews. Interview questions can guide group members to explore the spoken and unspoken rules of the group that may be contributing to conflicts. Questions such as "Whose rule is this?" or "What purpose does this rule serve and what would happen if it were broken?" can help the group members recognize unspoken rules, consider if a rule makes sense, and think about how it relates to their conflict.[77]

Intragroup conflict has received a great deal of attention from researchers and organizations that are interested in promoting effective teamwork. Teams, as we've all heard, are valued for their ability to develop innovative solutions to problems. The belief behind teams is that more

---

Conflict Quote ▼

When we look at the composition of teams within our company, we have found that those with a variety of perspectives are simply the most creative.

—Betsy Holden, Chief Executive Officer, Kraft Foods[74] ▲

talent at the table will generate more ideas and more wisdom will be available to evaluate them. But the teamwork ideal is about more than just adding together individual talents; rather, it is the synergy of teams that produces outcomes beyond the sum of the individual contributions.

Of course, the desired effect is not always the actual result. Most of us who have worked on teams know that unpleasant team experiences with mediocre outcomes are all too common-place. Teams are often wrought with conflict that limits their ability to produce. Organizations contribute to this conflict by creating teams with ambiguous goals and no clear purpose. They may also create teams that have more members than are required to do the job. Members in these groups will easily recognize that if they contribute very little to the group, the consequences will be minor. They may feel disconnected from the group because their contribution doesn't seem vital for the group's success. This arrangement can also encourage what is called "social loaf-ing," wherein a member of a group contributes little and allows the rest of the group to carry the weight.[78]

Organizations can help reduce this sort of intragroup conflict by clarifying the purpose and goals of teams and making them no larger than they need to be. In addition, organizations can help lessen team conflict by supporting teams with the resources they need. For example, a vir-tual team may be more effective if its organization provides the members with equipment for video or web conferencing. In addition, organizations can provide their employees with training on working in teams. Research has shown that having even one trained member on a team sig-nificantly improves outcomes. For groups, process determines outcome, and if groups have no tools in the form of techniques for managing meetings, the group is likely to spend time decid-ing and redeciding how things should be done, leading to frustration and conflict. Training can provide the team with these valuable tools.

IDENTIFYING FACTORS IN EMPLOYEE CONFLICTS

Managers can spend a great deal of their valuable time addressing employee conflicts or dealing with their fallout. But it is a mistake for managers to become involved in *all* employee conflicts. Before taking any action, managers must determine if the conflict is constructive or destructive. *Constructive conflict* is desirable, and though it may warrant monitoring to ensure that it doesn't spiral into a *destructive conflict,* it should be left alone. For managers dealing with destructive conflicts among employees, one of the important judgments they will need to make is determin-ing whether there is a business problem associated with the conflict and, if so, what it is. Identi-fying the business problem can help a manager gauge the need for intervention, prioritize the issues, and evaluate potential strategies for resolving the conflict. Managers must also identify the important parties (or *stakeholders*) in the conflict, the level of interdependence between them, and any situational or structural factors that may be contributing to the conflict. It can be helpful to use a guide such as the one in Table 2-4.

It is possible that through this process a manager may think of a solution to the problem that does not involve bringing the parties together to meet. For example, two departments that share a resource may produce a need that exceeds the resource's capacity, creating conflict. If more of the resource is made available, then the conflict is solved. This sort of solution could potentially be produced without even interviewing the parties individually.

An interview with the conflicting parties will be essential for solving more complex issues or serious conflicts. It's also necessary when simply solving the business problem isn't enough

Table 2-4   Guide for Analyzing Employee Conflicts

The Parties	Analysis of Conflict	Notes
Level of Conflict:	■ Who are the parties? ■ What level of conflict is this? ■ Are special considerations necessary given the level of conflict? If so, have these been addressed at the organizational level?	
Personality and Style:	■ What is known about the personalities of the parties that would contribute to the conflict? ■ What conflict management styles have the parties demonstrated thus far? ■ Is it appropriate for the type of conflict and other circumstances?	
Relationship (The Physical and Psychological Context):	■ What is the relationship between the parties? ■ What is the nature of their interdependence? ■ How is power distributed between the parties? ■ How much trust exists between the parties?	
Structural Factors:	■ What are the primary stressors in the work environments of the parties? ■ Are there policies, procedures, or norms contributing to the conflict?	
Messages/ Feedback:	■ Is verbally aggressive language being used? ■ Are ineffective communication tactics being used? ■ Is the communication climate defensive? ■ What is being communicated nonverbally?	

because the conflict has become destructive and will continue, even when the substantive aspects of the conflict are solved. Managers may interview the parties separately to get a sense of the history of the conflict from each party's perspective. While a number of factors that may contribute to the conflict may not be explicitly stated in an interview, the way parties talk about a conflict can often reveal them. By talking to those involved, managers may discern the type of conflict, the parties' goals, the conflict management styles of the parties, and what outcomes would satisfy everyone involved.[79]

In addition to helping the manager better understand the conflict, an interview can help all parties think about their conflict and clarify the issues. In organizations, people can be at odds over any number of issues. Managers can help them determine which issues are most significant and help them focus on a limited number of issues at one time. Importantly from the manager's perspective, interviews can help focus the attention of the parties on the business problem that must be solved.

The most important thing for a manager to do during the interview is to listen. Questions should be open-ended and nondirective. An interview is an information-gathering session. It may be that the manager is able to recognize a solution to conflict during the interview, but that's not really the goal.

Here are some sample open-ended, nondirective questions for interviewing:

- So, tell me what's going on.
- Can you tell me how you got to this point?
- What happened next?
- How would you describe this relationship?
- What would you like to see happen here?
- Who has been involved in this situation to this point?
- Who do you think needs to be brought in on this?
- How do you think this person feels about this situation?

Other useful techniques can be employed to help people identify which issues are the most important. For conflict between groups, a simple procedure is to have the group members write down their ideas about the most important issues. The ideas are then collected and recorded on a flip chart without any information identifying the contributor of the idea. Then, all members at the meeting have a chance to discuss the ideas and seek clarification on the meaning of each idea. After the discussion, the ideas are ranked in order of importance.[81]

This technique requires that the conflicting groups be in the presence of each other and communicate about their ideas. If the two groups are extremely hostile, the *Delphi Technique* could be used. This approach minimizes face-to-face communication between the groups during the time that issues are being identified. The Delphi Technique involves several steps and is most easily employed if a neutral person is available to facilitate the process. It begins with all the people involved writing out answers to open-ended questions about the issues as they see them. These answers are collected by the neutral person and read for themes. A summary of the ideas that emerge are then distributed to all participants, along with a questionnaire that asks them to respond to each idea according to some specified criteria. Those responses are then collected and a summary of the responses is created and distributed. Persons are asked if they would like to revise their position on the issues in light of this new information or if they would like to justify their position. These responses are collected and again a summary of them is created and distributed. The participants then give their final ranking. The process takes the parties from a general to specific definition of the most important issues without requiring them to be in the same room before the issue is well defined.[82]

At this point, managers will have a clear enough understanding of their employees' conflict to determine whether collaborative communication between the parties is the best path to a solution. Managers must also determine if they themselves can guide the parties to a resolution or if the help of a professional third party, such as a mediator, is needed. These options will be discussed in Chapter 3.

ANALYZING YOUR OWN CONFLICTS

In some ways, analyzing our own conflicts can be more difficult than analyzing employee conflicts. The main complication is our subjectivity. We know our side of the story. We see the situation from our perspective. In addition, we are more likely to be emotionally involved in our own conflicts, making it even more difficult to analyze them objectively. Because we interpret events through the biases of our own perceptions, understanding our tendencies and predispositions can only help us better understand our conflicts. True understanding of our own personal conflicts requires a true understanding of ourselves. Sometimes we find ourselves upset by something or in conflict with someone, and we don't really understand why. Occasionally, we may find that a conflict has more to do with something about ourselves than the behavior of the other party.

So how do we get to know ourselves better? In his book, *Listening to Conflict,* Erik Van Slyke talks about interpersonal zones for people to explore when learning about themselves. He recommends paying particular attention to our *comfort zones* and *hot zones.* Most of us are familiar with the term **comfort zone** and know this refers to being in a situation where we are comfortable, at ease, and confident. A **hot zone** is outside our comfort zone, where we experience anxiety or strong negative emotions. Research shows that when we have strong emotions, we will look around our environment to find reasons for them. That means that sometimes simply being outside our comfort zone can contribute to conflict. Inside a hot zone, you may feel stressed, mentally exhausted, frustrated, or even helpless. Knowing what triggers these emotions in you can help you when you analyze your own conflicts. Many times, underlying a conflict is a hot zone.[83]

Other interpersonal zones that Van Slyke recommends exploring include *values zones, social zones,* and *cognitive zones.* **Values zones** are created by our beliefs about what is important and what is right or wrong. Knowing what we value and how to prioritize our values can help us to avoid frustration, ineffectiveness in life, and mistakes, as well as help us to understand and possibly avoid certain conflicts. In organizations, groups or individuals in conflict inevitably have different values at the top of their values priority lists. For example, research and development may value speed and innovation, while accounting may value detail and routine. Knowing how we prioritize our values is important, and living in a way that reflects that prioritization can improve the overall quality of our lives and help us to avoid a great deal of intrapersonal and interpersonal conflict.[84]

Social zones refer to our preferences and tendencies regarding social interaction. People vary in interpersonal needs such as the need for affection, the need to be included in social groups, and the need to control others. One common distinction among social interaction preferences is extroversion versus introversion. Extroverts thrive on interactions with others, while introverts are drained by them.

Cognitive zones refer to our preferred strategies for dealing with information. Some people prefer facts, details, logic, and pragmatism and use an analytic strategy for evaluating information. On the other hand, some people prefer principles, summaries, instincts, and flexibility and use an empathic strategy for evaluating information that is people-oriented and subjective.

Knowing about our interpersonal zones can help us recognize when we are reacting to one of our zones rather than the actual behavior of another person.[85] Imagine an introvert and an extrovert working together on a project. One needs to be alone to think, the other has to be talking to someone to develop ideas. The extrovert may have a high need for inclusion and control, while the introvert may want to limit the relationship to the project only and to have more independence. This combination could make for a great deal of conflict, but much of it would be about different interpersonal preferences rather than about issues. In a situation of this sort, time might be spent trying to solve conflicts by changing the other person. If the introvert and extrovert understood their own preferences better, they would be less likely to interpret different choices as a source of conflict.

Conflict Quote ▼

The trick is to reframe the situation in your mind and to focus on the things that you can control.
—Paul Stoltz, Organizational Consultant[86] ▲

To analyze any particular conflict, we might begin by considering the conflict history. A major difficulty with considering what happened is that we only have one side of the story. We know our perceptions of the events surrounding the conflict, but we don't know the perceptions of the other party. When we analyze the history of the conflict, we can begin to balance our view by asking ourselves a few questions.

- **What was our contribution to this conflict?** Typically, when we think about our conflicts, we blame others for their part. But few conflicts are the result of only one party's actions. Considering our contribution to the problem, as well as that of the other party, increases our power to change the outcomes in the future.[87]

- **Are we trying to interpret events using beliefs that don't really work for us?** We all have belief systems, which we use to interpret our world. These may include beliefs that we have held for a very long time, perhaps since childhood, and validity of those beliefs may never have been examined. If we examine our beliefs, we may find some beliefs that contribute to our conflict are without foundation and which could, perhaps, be changed. A manager, for example, may hold the belief that *working mothers are unreliable employees.* This belief may affect the manager's decisions about assignments and promotions. Perhaps this belief is based on a previous experience with a working mother, but a generalization to all working mothers is not really warranted. The manager may examine the belief and determine that it needs to be updated or revised.

- **Are we making any unjustified inferences?** Perhaps we are making negative inferences about another party when they're not really warranted. For instance, "The quality of her work is poor" is an observation about behavior, but "She doesn't care about her job" is an inference that frames the behavior in a negative way. Alternatively, "There is something interfering with her performance" allows for many possible reasons for the behavior. During a conflict, an unjustified inference we frequently make is confusing impact with intention. Someone does something that has a negative impact on us and we conclude that the person's intent was to do us harm. But, very often, harming us was not the intention of the other party. That may not make the act any less harmful, but it does make it more likely that we can work through our conflict with that other person.[88]

- **What does the other person think happened?** We already know our perceptions, and trying to imagine the other person's perceptions can help us understand the conflict better and help us understand our own contributions. When we are involved in conflict, we think we are right and the other person is wrong. We must remember that the other person may very well feel the same way about us.[89]

While sorting through a conflict, we must also address our feelings. It is tempting to avoid the feelings issue, especially in a work context, but conflicts are by their very nature emotional events, some to a higher degree than others. Feelings can be at the very core of a conflict, and if we attempt to ignore them, our feelings may well leak out slowly or in an uncontrollable outburst. Furthermore, we are in poor condition to work through a conflict with the other person if our own feelings are hurt. Hurt feelings can interfere with our ability to listen well and certainly diminish our motivation to take the other person's view.[90]

Our feelings are often tied to identity issues we may experience during conflicts. When we are engaged in conflict, we may question what the conflict means to us in terms of how we see ourselves and how others see us. Conflicts can affect our feelings of competence and self-worth. These issues are often not openly expressed during a conflict and are frequently buried under more explicit concerns in the conflict. We may have to dig a little to understand them, but because conflicts that threaten our identities can feel very serious and send us into an emotional tailspin, understanding these issues can be important and beneficial.[91]

Understanding our conflicts also requires considering our goals and their related issues. Issues can be objective, as with content goals or process goals; or they can be personal, as with identity goals and relational goals. Objective issues tend to have less emotional arousal attached, but, if mishandled, these issues can quickly become personal. Personal issues usually involve more intense emotion. When conflicts involve personal issues and intense feelings, our goals may not be the ones we appear to be arguing about. We may, in fact, argue over a content goal when an identity goal or relational goal is the real source of trouble.[92]

Using a guide like the one offered for analyzing employee conflicts in Table 2-4 may be useful for ensuring that you consider those contributing factors in your analysis. However, your analysis of your own conflict can be more complete, since you have information about your perceptions and feelings that you wouldn't necessarily have about an employee. The guide in Table 2-5 may be a useful tool for analyzing your own conflicts.

As you begin to analyze *your* conflict, you will need to decide whether or not to raise the issue with the other party. By completely analyzing the conflict before raising the issue, you have an opportunity to prepare yourself to do so effectively. You also have the opportunity to determine if there is a better way to solve the problem. You may determine that the conflict is really the result of differences in interpersonal needs or unexamined beliefs. You may determine that the conflict is really more about your reaction to the other party rather than the behavior of the other party.

If you determine that an issue must be raised with someone else, you will benefit from possessing the communication tools needed to work through conflict collaboratively. Whether it is your conflict or the conflict of your employees, resolving it in a way that satisfies all parties and strengthens the relationship between them is only possible through effective communication. In the next chapter, we discuss specific techniques for communicating collaboratively to resolve conflicts.

Table 2-5   Analyzing Your own Conflicts

Questions to Ask Yourself	Notes
What do I think happened?	
What does the other person think happened?	
Which of my actions contributed to this conflict? (If you answer "none" to this question, begin reading this book over again.)	
What goals do I have at stake here? ▪ content ▪ process ▪ relational ▪ identity ▪ values	
Am I ignoring situational factors that may be contributing to this person's behavior?	
What are my feelings about this situation? Do my feelings seem appropriate given the goals I've identified? If not, what else is going on?	

DISCUSSION QUESTIONS

1. Do most conflicts occur at more than one level? Think of examples to support your answer.

2. One of the contributors to workplace conflict is the stress of having too much to do in too little time. In tight economic times, organizations may not be able to hire more workers to relieve the workload. What else can they do to relieve the stress the employees feel?

3. Discuss your current or previous place of employment in terms of the factors that contribute to conflict. What about the organization contributed to conflict and what about it helped prevent conflict?

4. Why do employees of low power express their conflicts indirectly? What is the danger of this type of expression for the organization? What can managers do to encourage a more constructive means of dealing with conflict?

5. If you are in a conflict, is it possible to influence the conflict management style that the other party is using? How could you do so?

6. Is it easier to analyze your own conflicts or the conflicts of your employees? Explain your answer.

7. Under what circumstances would you consider it best not to raise an issue with another party? Would you ever suggest to an employee that he or she not raise an issue? When and why? What impact, if any, would you expect that advice to have on the employee's feelings about you and the organization?

ENDNOTES

1. Douglas Stone, Bruce Patton, and Sheila Heen, *Difficult Conversations* (New York: Viking, 1999).
2. William Wilmot and Joyce Hocker, *Interpersonal Conflict,* 6th ed. (New York: McGraw-Hill Higher Education, 2001).
3. Stephen W. Littlejohn and Kathy Domenici, *Engaging Communication in Conflict* (Thousand Oaks, CA: Sage, 2001).
4. Wilmot and Hocker.
5. Littlejohn and Domenici.
6. Robert P. Vecchio, *Organizational Behavior,* 3rd ed. (Fort Worth, TX: Dryden Press, 1995), 473–480.
7. Kurt Lewin, *A Dynamic Theory of Personality* (New York: McGraw-Hill, 1935).
8. Vecchio.
9. Michael D. Ensley, Allison W. Pearson, and Allen C. Amason, "Understanding the Dynamics of New Venture Top Management Teams: Cohesion, Conflict, and New Venture Performance," *Journal of Business Venturing,* 17 (2002): 365–386.
10. Robert Bacal, "Conflict and Cooperation in the Workplace," 1998. Available at Institute for Conflict Prevention web site, http://www.work911.com/articles.htm.
11. Karen A. Jehn and Elizabeth A. Mannix, "The Dynamic Nature of Conflict: A Longitudinal Study of Intragroup Conflict and Group Performance," *Academy of Management Journal,* 44 (2001): 238–251.
12. Leslie A. DeChurch and Michelle A. Marks, "Maximizing the Benefits of Task Conflict: The Role of Conflict Management," *The International Journal of Conflict Management,* 12 (2001): 4–22.
13. M. Afzalur Rahim, *Managing Conflict in Organizations,* 2nd ed. (Westport, CT: Praeger, 1992).
14. Kristin Bihary, Eaton Corporation, telephone interview, Cleveland, OH, February 26, 2003.
15. Hutchinson, S., telephone interview, December 18, 2002. Integra Realty Resources, Inc., New York, NY. The random telephone survey of 1,206 working adults in the continental U.S. has a margin of error of plus or minus 3%, and was conducted with the assistance of Opinion Research Corporation International of Princeton, N.J. The study was conducted November 8 to November 12, 2001.
16. Jennifer Daw, "Road Rage, Air Rage, and Now 'Desk Rage,'" *Monitor on Psychology,* July/August (2001): 53.
17. Carol Hymowitz and Rachel Emma Silverman, "Can Workplace Stress Get Worse?" *The Wall Street Journal,* January 16, 2001, B1, Column 2 and B4, Column 3.
18. Integra Realty Resources.
19. Jennifer Wirth, "Ban Office Romance, Many Say," *The Cincinnati Enquirer,* November 25, 2002. Online Edition at http://www.enquirer.com.
20. Hymowitz and Silverman.
21. Gary W. Evans, "Behavioral and Physiological Consequences of Crowding in Humans," *Journal of Applied Social Psychology,* 9 (1979): 27–46.
22. Nissen, Beth. "Overworked, overwrought: 'Desk rage' at work," CNN.com, November 15, 2000.
23. Russell Wild, "Risky Rewards," *Working Woman,* June 2001, 77.
24. Wild.
25. Annie Finnigan, "Different Strokes," *Working Woman,* April 2001, 42–46.
26. John Ford, "Cross Cultural Conflict Resolution in Teams," October 2001. Available: http://www.mediate.com.

27. Ford.
28. Ibid.
29. J. R. P. French and B. H. Raven, "The Bases of Personal Power," in *Group Dynamics,* edited by J. D. Cartwright and A. Zander (Evanston, IL: Row, Peterson, 1962), 607–622.
30. Wilmot and Hocker.
31. Ibid.
32. Ibid.
33. Willem F. G. Mastenbroek, *Conflict Management and Organization Development* (Chichester, England: Wiley, 1993).
34. Mastenbroek.
35. John Ford, "Dealing with Difficult Behavior," December 2001. Available: http://www .mediate.com.
36. Mastenbroek.
37. Ibid.
38. Ibid.
39. Steven A. Beebe, Susan J. Beebe, and Mark V. Redmond, *Interpersonal Communication: Relating to Others* (Boston: Allyn and Bacon, 1999).
40. Daniel Goleman, *Working with Emotional Intelligence* (New York: Bantam Books, 1998).
41. Erik J. Van Slyke, *Listening to Conflict: Finding Constructive Solutions to Workplace Disputes* (New York: Amacom, 1999).
42. Susan Fritz, William F. Brown, Joyce P. Lunde, and Elizabeth Banset, *Interpersonal Skills for Leadership* (Upper Saddle River, NJ: Prentice Hall, 1999).
43. Wilmot and Hocker.
44. Ibid.
45. Ibid.
46. Ibid.
47. Rahim.
48. Wilmot and Hocker.
49. Ibid.
50. Ibid.
51. Rahim.
52. Wilmot and Hocker.
53. Rahim.
54. Lourdes Munduate, Juan Ganaza, José Peiro, and Martin Euwema, "Patterns of Styles in Conflict Management and Effectiveness," *The International Journal of Conflict Management,* 10 (1999): 5–24.
55. Rahim.
56. Wilmot and Hocker.
57. Ibid.
58. Dean Keith Simonton, "Personality and Politics," in *Handbook of Personality Theory and Research,* edited by Lawrence A. Pervin (New York: Guilford Press, 1990), 670–692.
59. Paul Falcone, "When Employees Have a 'Tude," *HR Magazine,* 46 (June 2001): 189–194.
60. Wilmot and Hocker.
61. Sharon S. Brehm, *Intimate Relationships,* 2nd. ed. (New York: McGraw-Hill, 1992).
62. A. Mehrabian, *Nonverbal Communication* (Chicago: Aldine-Atherton, 1972).
63. J. Larry Goff and Roy A. Cook, "Coming of Age with Self-Managed Teams: Dealing with a Problem Employee," *Journal of Business and Psychology,* 16 (2002): 485–496.
64. Alex Thio, *Sociology* (New York: Longman, 1998).
65. Thio.
66. Rahim.

67. Linda L. Putnam, "Communication and Interpersonal Conflict in Organizations," *Management Communication Quarterly,* 1 (1988): 293–301.
68. Wilmot and Hocker.
69. Michael Billig and Henri Tajfel, "Social Categorization and Similarity in Intergroup Behavior," *European Journal of Social Psychology,* 3 (1973): 27–52.
70. Melanie L. Harrington, "Diversity or Diversion?" *Black Enterprise,* 32, issue 12 (July 2002).
71. Rahim.
72. Muzafer Sherif, O. J. Harvey, B. Jack White, William R. Hood, and Carolyn W. Sherif, *The Robbers Cave Experiment: Intergroup Conflict and Cooperation* (Middletown, CT: Wesleyan University Press, 1988).
73. Diane Vaughan, *The Challenger Launch Decision* (Chicago: University of Chicago Press, 1996).
74. Finnigan.
75. Ensley, Pearson, and Amason.
76. Wilmot and Hocker.
77. Ibid.
78. Bibb Latane, Kipling Williams, and Stephen Harkins, "Many Hands Make Light the Work: The Causes and Consequences of Social Loafing," *Journal of Personality and Social Psychology,* 37 (1979): 822–832.
79. Daniel Dana, *Conflict Resolution* (New York: McGraw-Hill, 2001).
80. Ford, "Dealing with Difficult Behavior."
81. Wilmot and Hocker.
82. Myra Warren Isenhart and Michael Spangle, *Collaborative Approaches to Resolving Conflict* (Thousand Oaks, CA: Sage, 2000).
83. Van Slyke.
84. Ibid.
85. Ibid.
86. Cheryl Dahle, "Don't Get Mad—Get over It!" *Fast Company,* vol. 22, February 1999, http://www.fastcompany.com/online/22/toolbox.html.
87. Van Slyke.
88. Stone, Patton, and Heen.
89. Ibid.
90. Ibid.
91. Ibid.
92. Wilmot and Hocker.

3 WORKING THROUGH CONFLICT

In many instances, working through conflict can be fairly simple. For example, conflicts over content goals that do not represent a large loss or gain for either party can often be resolved without the complication of intense emotions. Cognitive conflicts between people with unimportant or temporary relationships can be ended quickly by the more powerful of them, even if the less powerful of the two isn't happy with the solution. But when conflicts are complex, when relationships matter, or when it's important that all parties be satisfied with the resolution, working through conflicts can be involved and challenging.

THREE ALTERNATIVES

It may seem a bit simplistic, but you have three basic alternatives for dealing with conflict. First, you can try to change the other person. This process usually involves getting the other person to accept that he or she is at fault and needs to change. As attractive as this strategy is, it's usually unsuccessful. As you read in Chapter 2, people rarely agree to being labeled as "the problem," nor do they welcome the efforts of others to "fix" them.[1]

A second option is to attempt to alter the conflict conditions. A change to any of the conflict elements will have a resulting effect on the conflict. If you and a co-worker are in conflict over a scarce resource, you could increase the availability of the resource. If your department and another are heavily interdependent and are in conflict, you could reduce the level of interdependence. Changes such as these, however, are sometimes difficult, if not impossible, to accomplish and in many cases are simply not enough to solve the problem.[2]

The third alternative is to change yourself. When you are involved in a conflict, *you* become one of the conflict elements, and if you change, the conflict will change. If you are motivated and willing, you can change your perceptions of and communication about the conflict. If you have always thought of the guy down the hall as a total jerk, with whom you have nothing in common but the need to work together, you can rethink your opinion of him. You can explore the reasons why he might behave like a jerk (other than actually being one). In addition to changing your perception, you can change your communication. Instead of calling this fellow names, you can use more neutral language and talk about him as someone you want to learn to work with.[3]

But, as you may have guessed, this alternative is difficult for a number of reasons. First, it's difficult because it requires self-change, and as most of us know from experience, changing ourselves can be tough. Second, it's difficult because you are agreeing to change before the other party does. You stop calling the guy down the hall a jerk, but he, at least for a while, will still call you a ninny. It can be tough to be the first to change, but the risk can be well worth the effort.[4]

Sometimes a change in your own perception is all that's needed to effectively resolve a conflict. Two friends who do not work together were talking about their places of employment. One friend shared her continual annoyance with her co-workers for leaving their dirty coffee cups in the break-room sink at night. She interpreted that as a sign of laziness and lack of respect for the workplace. The other friend observed that at her workplace several people also left their coffee cups in the sink at night—and she was one of them. She said that she was always in a hurry to catch the train after work and so waited until morning to wash her cup before reusing it. After that brief conversation, the friend who was annoyed about the unwashed cups changed her view of the problem and (remarkably) was no longer bothered by them.

In this chapter, we will begin by reviewing techniques for working through your own conflicts once you have decided to raise a conflict issue. We'll look at dialogue and collaborative communication to build relationships while working through conflicts. And we'll describe communication tools that can be used to accomplish this objective, specifically, the collaborative mindset, effective listening and feedback, and positive language (see Table 3-1). We will then explore how managers can act as mediators to help employees work through their conflicts and examine options for bringing in a professional third party when manager-mediation is inappropriate or when a conflict is more than a manager can handle.

Table 3-1   Communication Tools for Dialogue and Collaboration

Communication Tools

The Collaborative Mindset
- An attitude of curiosity
- Separating people from their position
- A focus on interests

Effective Listening and Feedback
- Asking questions
- Reflective listening
- Nonverbal immediacy cues
- Dealing with emotions

Positive Language
- Reframing
- Relational statements
- Specific behavioral statements

RAISING AN ISSUE

Moving out of avoidance by raising an issue allows people to share important information about each other and the situation they find themselves in, including complaints that others may be completely unaware of. Raising an issue allows people to communicate about the importance of their relationship and attempt to change something they feel should be changed. Only if you raise an issue can you produce a solution with the participation of all parties.[5]

When the objective for raising an issue is resolving a conflict constructively, the very act of doing so can create possibilities for improved relationships by addressing problems rather than letting them quietly escalate. If the point of raising an issue, however, is to convince the other person that she is wrong, to make her feel bad, to admit guilt, or to apologize, the outcome may not be satisfactory to either of you.

Conflict Quote ▼

People don't learn by staring into a mirror; people learn by encountering difference. So, hand-in-hand with the courage to face reality comes the courage to surface and orchestrate conflicts.
    —Ronald Heifetz, Director, Leadership Education Project at Harvard University[6] ▲

Being clear about your goal beforehand is crucial for determining your approach when raising an issue. The experience of Melissa Giovagnoli, a highly sought-after speaker and trainer, provides a case in point. She had agreed to be the keynote speaker for a conference at a subsidiary of optics manufacturer Canon. Just four days before the engagement, the company canceled her speech in an effort to reduce spending. Giovagnoli was understandably upset. "I'll have to eat more than 20 hours of prep time. And I turned down another assignment for this," she thought. At first she considered contacting the company and demanding compensation for the time she had put in. But before she acted, she thought about what that would get her. She would be angry and she would make the company angry. "If I had pointed my finger at them and said, 'You did this to me,' I would have put them on the defensive," says Giovagnoli. Instead, she thought about her long-term goal. If she focused on the immediate content goal, it might be at the expense of any long-term relationship goal. In the end, she called the company and talked to them about how the relationship could be saved. They were able to negotiate a new speaking deal at a lower fee, with some follow-up consulting.[7]

When a conflict is complex, you improve your chances of achieving your goal when raising an issue if you prepare by analyzing the conflict and considering the contributing factors, as we suggested in Chapter 2. Content or substantive issues tend to be the most obvious but may be only a minor part of the conflict. Process, relational, or identity issues may be involved as well. (The involvement of these issues is especially likely when the relationship between the parties is important.) You can manage yourself better—particularly your emotions—during interactions with the other person if you do some advance thinking about the true nature of the conflict, your own feelings, and the probable feelings of the other person.

COLLABORATIVE COMMUNICATION AND DIALOGUE

PROTECTING RELATIONSHIPS DURING CONFLICTS

In most cases, despite whatever initial reaction we may have to a conflict, we are interested in preserving our relationship with the other party. Important relationships in an organizational setting can take a number of forms, many of which have nothing to do with friendship or liking. They can be based exclusively on interdependence, for example. If an important relationship is functioning effectively, it can be considered a healthy working relationship. Successful relationships at work, like all other relationships, experience conflict. People who work together will always have differences. In successful relationships, people simply develop ways to deal with them. Co-workers may resolve some issues and agree to disagree about others, but they are still able to work together well. A successful working relationship means that the parties treat each other with respect and are able to function within the organization, despite their differences.[8]

During conflict, we are often so focused on the substantive issues and the goal of reaching a settlement that we fail to think about the process we use to get there or what that will do to the relationship. But this is a mistake. How we go about resolving a conflict in an ongoing association can affect the relationship either positively or negatively. For example, a competing or dominating style that leads to personal attacks, threats, or other coercive techniques can leave relationships damaged, while collaborative problem solving can help a relationship grow. We want, in most cases, to maintain successful working relationships with others in our organization—even those who may be in conflict with us. Thus, the importance of the relationship is a consideration when deciding how to work through the conflict. When a relationship is particularly important to us, we must continually keep in mind the process we use for working through conflict.[9]

This approach might seem to suggest that we should automatically become accommodating when we are in a conflict with another person who is important to us, if only for the sake of the relationship. But accommodation isn't always the best choice. Relationships built on one-sided concessions can be fragile, and agreements that are not in the best interest of one can lead to resentment toward the other. Working through conflict constructively, rather than accommodating, can build and strengthen relationships. Constructive conflict resolution encourages people to accept each other as a person of value, even during conflict.[10]

Working through conflict constructively is the result of effective communication. In so many ways, we create our worlds and construct our realities through communication. Communication is at the center of how we express, maintain, and resolve our conflicts. How we talk about our differences is what makes conflict constructive—or destructive. Plainly put, the communication we use in the conflict resolution process will determine the content and relational outcomes that we achieve.

During conflict, we can speak about winning, fighting for our rights, or getting what we deserve, and being in the right. We can also talk about blame and fault. We can speak about our options as if they were limited and our position as if it were the only one that would do. All of which will create a competitive win/lose environment and can lead to dissatisfying outcomes and damaged relationships. Alternatively, we can talk about perceptions and contribution, rather than blame. We can talk about creative options, innovative solutions, working together, and collaborative problem solving. All of which create an environment for constructive conflict.[11]

USING DIALOGUE TO ACHIEVE COMMUNICATION OBJECTIVES

Communication strategies used in the conflict resolution process should accomplish several things, including communicating caring, promoting understanding, saving face, and managing emotions. However, even in the absence of verbal aggression and disrespectful nonverbal mannerisms, we can still face barriers to accomplishing these communication goals during conflict. Three important barriers include:[12]

- **Not listening.** We often assume there is no need to listen to other people, that we know all we need to about how they view things. In contrast, we are quite likely to assume that others could learn a great deal from us.
- **Communicating in one direction.** We tend to approach conflict in the "tell" mode. We want communication to flow in one direction, with us telling others what we think they did wrong, what they need to know about how we see things, and what they need to change.
- **Sending mixed messages.** In addition, we frequently send mixed messages. In most conflicts, we often have more than one emotion, several constituencies to satisfy, and various goals we are trying to meet, which can lead us to send mixed messages that complicate the issue and confuse other people.

Using dialogue can help us overcome communication barriers and accomplish our communication goals. Dialogue is more than a conversation between two people. It is an approach to communication characterized by acceptance, genuineness, and an effort to fully understand and empathize with the other person.[13] While poor communication can damage relationships, dialogue is a form of communication that respects relationships. It honors individuals and differences in perspective. Through dialogue, people attempt to get to know each other's perspectives and look at things from another frame of reference. It makes it possible for each to explore differences and commonalities. It also allows the meaning that is being constructed through the communication of each person to come to light.[14]

THE COLLABORATIVE MINDSET

DEVELOP AN ATTITUDE OF CURIOSITY

The dialogue process contributes to successful outcomes in conflict resolution because it enables people to understand each other better. Conflicts are about perceptions, and understanding perceptions is vital to working through them successfully. By comparison, objective reality may be of little help in resolving our differences. Imagine, for example, that you meet with a new prospect. He calls to reject your pitch on a day when you aren't available. He insists on speaking to someone that day and the co-worker who takes his call talks him into a deal. You and your co-worker may agree on the objective reality of these events and still not agree on how the commission should be split. To work through such conflicts we have to develop an attitude of true curiosity about the other person's perspective.[15]

Only with clear understanding of each other's perceptions and concerns can people in conflict work collaboratively to produce a satisfying solution. When we initially analyze a conflict, we think about the problem and try to understand the contributing factors. But at that point, we still have just one side of the story: our own. The true nature of the conflict and possible solutions may not emerge until we communicate openly with the other party. Effective communication allows each of us to explore the other's perspectives and to attempt to create a third perspective that both may share. From this perspective, it is easier for each of us to try to discover what the other person's true interests may be.

But dialogue is neither simple nor easy. It requires a willingness to spend time exploring the other person's point of view. It necessitates a commitment to taking turns listening at a deeper level. It means using language that saves face and asking questions that further the interaction and our own understanding. It's a risky process because it requires us to explore unfamiliar points of view. We may learn that we were wrong or that we did not have all the information we needed when we acted. We may see that, from another person's frame of reference, we contributed greatly to the conflict.[16]

Dialogue also requires an investment of time and energy that we typically wouldn't make unless the relationship were somehow important to us. When we create dialogue, we communicate our acceptance and understanding of other people and our caring for them. This is not the same thing as communicating that we agree with them or that we are accommodating them. Rather, we are simply recognizing their value as people and working to understand them.

Conflict Quote ▼

We generally do not look at conflict as opportunity—we tend to think about conflict as unpleasant, counter-productive and time-consuming. Conflict that occurs in organizations need not be destructive, provided the energy associated with conflict is harnessed and directed towards problem-solving and organizational improvement.

—Robert Bacal, Institute for Conflict Prevention[17] ▲

SEPARATING PEOPLE FROM THEIR POSITIONS

Only if we develop an attitude of true curiosity will we be willing to take the risk and invest the energy required for dialogue. When we really want to know another person's perspective, it shows. But adding to the challenge of dialogue is our tendency to see the other party in the conflict as the problem. Blaming others for conflict does not help solve the problem, even when we feel the blame is justified. Neither does making negative inferences about other people and their motives.

Sometimes we may feel as if the other person views *us* as the problem. We may read something negative into a person's comments, or we may feel as if we are being personally attacked if someone points out an error we've made. We may think another person doesn't like us if he or she opposes our suggestion.[18] And it may be that the other party *does* see us as the problem. Keep in mind that other people's perceptions about how things are in a conflict may vary markedly from our own, and, perhaps, if we viewed the situation from their frame of reference, we would see things just as they do.[19]

Unquestionably, it's hard to engage in dialogue and feel curious about another person's perspective and interests if we think that person really *is* the problem, doesn't like us, or isn't treating us fairly. We need to separate the people from the problem. In other words, we need to focus on troubling behaviors as the problem and not the people or personalities involved. We can work toward separating people issues from the other issues in two ways: First, by recognizing the difference between intentions and impact. And second, by thinking about our conflict as a problem for the relationship that people must solve together, rather than as problems for individuals who must compete to get the best solution for themselves.[20]

Recognizing the difference between impact and intentions can make it much easier for us to think positively about the other party in a conflict. Often, when people do things that hurt us or make us angry, that wasn't really their intention. Recognizing also that the negative consequences we are experiencing are probably unintended can help us to see the problem and the person as separate. Of course, this doesn't make the damage any less significant, but it can help control the damage to the relationship.[21]

FOCUSING ON INTERESTS

With traditional conflict resolution approaches, people argue their *positions* rather than their *interests*. A party's interests are their true concerns. For example, two managers may disagree

---

A CASE IN POINT: WINNING TEAMS LEARN TO MANAGE RELATIONSHIPS

Ernesto Bertarelli, the Swiss biotech billionaire who won the America's Cup—the Holy Grail of international yachting—has never been short of either ambition or ego. He promised to bring the cup back to Europe for the first time since the Americans carried it off in 1851. And he's promised to hoist the trophy atop Switzerland's 13,500-foot Matterhorn as a gesture of defiance to those who said he couldn't win it.

His team *Alinghi's* 5–0 victory in the 2003 sailing match in New Zealand's Hauraki Gulf was the result of more than grand ambition or a large bankroll, however. Much of Bertarelli's success came from his ability to identify and hire the world's best blue water sailors and to manage the egos that come with such skill. Russell Coutts, the skipper who had helped win the cup for New Zealand in 1999, credits Bertarelli's business skill and conflict management abilities for much of their success.

"Ernesto has been absolutely key in the process because he was able to bring a lot of lessons from his business," says Mr. Coutts. "He has a wealth of experience in bringing people together from different countries and cultures and getting them to work effectively."

Mr. Bertarelli may look like a playboy type—he loves sailing big boats, he is married to a former Eng-lish beauty queen, and he superstitiously calls all his yachts *Alinghi* because it brings him good luck. But he is also a very able manager. He selected his team nearly three years ago and delegated operational management to Mr. Coutts and Michel Bonnefous, a sailing colleague.

By contrast, Larry Ellison, the Oracle chief executive and losing competitor to Bertarelli in the Louis Vuitton Challenge Cup series, hired four of the world's best skippers, interfered in their decision making, and his boat was riven by internal tensions. The last skipper aboard *Oracle,* in fact, sacked Ellison—threw him off the boat.

"In the cup we have a rule that you have to choose your people at the beginning and then cannot change them," says Mr. Bertarelli. "I think that is one of the most important decisions anyone has ever to make, be it in business or in competition—choose your people right."

Source: W. Hall, "Swiss Billionaire Reaches the Pinnacle of Sailing Success," *Financial Times,* Monday, March 3, 2003, 14. See also: W. Hall and G. Dyer, "America's Cup: Playboy Gets Serious," http://www.financialtimes.com, February 26, 2003; http://www.americascup.yahoo.com.

about assigning a particular employee to lead a project team. One manager may be concerned that the employee's department will fall behind in its work if the employee is pulled away for the project. So this manager's interest is the employee's department staying caught up in its work. His position would be to not appoint the employee as team leader. The other manager's interest may be in rewarding the employee for stellar performance with a position of leadership. Her position would be to appoint the employee as team leader.

Any interest may have multiple positions that can satisfy it. However, when people argue their positions, they tend to lock into just one position, usually the most obvious, and argue as if only that position is an acceptable solution to the conflict. In our preceding example, if the managers had stayed focused on their positions, they would have argued back and forth about whether or not to appoint the employee and would never have agreed. Instead, they focused on their interests and found multiple, mutually acceptable solutions to their conflict. They eventually decided to appoint the employee and bring a temporary worker into the department if it were to get behind. They also thought about rewarding the employee in other ways and discussed appointing someone else as team leader.

When people argue their positions, their true interests may be hard to recognize. Furthermore, their positions may be about substantive issues, ignoring any relational, identity, or process goals. Engaging in dialogue can help parties communicate openly about interests rather than positions and make possible the production of mutually satisfying solutions through collaborative problem solving.[22]

EFFECTIVE LISTENING AND FEEDBACK

Sharing each other's perceptions is only as effective as the listening skills of the parties involved. Effective listening is an integral part of the dialogue process. Dialogue requires **empathic listening** or listening at the deepest level. Empathic listening goes well beyond just hearing what is said. When listening empathically, the listener tries to take the perspective of the speaker.

Listening well during a conflict requires a serious effort to overcome the common barriers to effective listening, including removing distractions, paying attention, maintaining eye contact, and not interrupting. But good listening during conflict is even more challenging for several reasons. Emotions may be running high. People may be reluctant to share important information because trust may be low or they may become defensive. Listening empathically is one way to build trust. When people listen to others without becoming defensive or shutting them down, speakers will be more likely to open up and share their perspectives. We can improve our ability to listen during conflicts by using active listening techniques, dealing effectively with emotions, and using appropriate nonverbal communication.

ASKING QUESTIONS

Some people may need encouragement to share their perspectives. Asking them to share their side with us first by using an open-ended question can get things started. If we are nonthreatening and listen well, the person will begin to feel more at ease and speak more freely. We can encourage the flow of information by asking more open-ended, probing questions such as:

- Can you tell me more about that?
- How do you feel about that?
- What did that mean for you?
- How do you see that?

We must be careful when asking questions to further a person's disclosure to avoid phrasing the questions in ways that will put that person on the defensive. Questions that start with "why" or "how could you" often push the respondent into a defensive state. We also want to avoid asking leading questions, or questions that are really statements phrased as a question ("Isn't it true that. . . ?"). Questions can be phrased in ways that carefully disguise the ego attack contained within them. Obviously, we want to avoid asking questions of this type as well.

Here is a sampling of questions to avoid:

- Why did you do that?
- How could you believe that?
- Don't you think that's right?
- Wouldn't this way be better?
- Surely you can recognize the error, can't you?
- But certainly you must agree with that decision, don't you?

Once a person begins disclosing his or her perspective, we as listeners want to make sure we understand what's being said by asking clarifying questions. Nonjudgmental, clarifying questions allow us to get more information about a point we don't fully understand and check our perceptions of the other person's message for accuracy.

- Can you tell me more about that?
- Could you give me an example of what you mean by that?
- Do you mean. . . ?
- Is what you're saying. . . ?

Questions about the future can also be helpful. First, they help us clarify our understanding of what the other party wants as an outcome. Second, they keep us focused on what can be changed rather than finding fault and laying blame for what has already happened. Questions such as, "What can we do differently next time this occurs?" are optimistic and empower each of us to create change.[24]

REFLECTIVE LISTENING

Another way to check our perceptions of another person's message is to use reflective listening. **Reflective listening** is a technique in which the listener reflects, or repeats, back to the speaker the content of the message, the feelings behind the message, and the conclusions of the message. This doesn't mean that the listener parrots exactly what the speaker has said. Rather, the listener is stating in his or her own words what has been communicated.

Consider a situation in which one manager is upset with another for changing the date of a meeting with an important client. The following exchange is, of course, a highly simplified example that lacks the richness and complexity of real life and is meant only to illustrate reflecting content, feelings, and conclusions.

> *Person 1: You moved that meeting to the 22nd without checking with me. I just got done scheduling an onsite visit with another client for that day, and now I'm going to have to call them back and change those plans. I don't think that makes me—or the company— look very good.*

> *Person 2: Sorry about that. I moved the meeting to a day you already had booked (reflecting content). I don't blame you for being irritated with me (reflecting feeling). I really put you in an awkward position with our other clients, and that could have been avoided if I had checked with you before moving the meeting (reflecting conclusions).*

DEALING WITH EMOTIONS

Reflecting feelings while listening is manageable when our emotions are in check, but what happens when they get out of control? Both substantive and relational issues can be laden with emotion—the more important the issues, the more intense the emotions. While some emotions can be useful because they motivate us to do something about a conflict, strong feelings that go unaddressed can make conversation—especially dialogue—difficult. It's hard to see things from another person's perspective if we are consumed with anger or hurt.[25]

Conflict is often associated with feelings of anger and fear. When we feel that we've been wronged or threatened, as we often do during conflict, we will likely feel angry or fearful. We all know that people don't enjoy feeling angry and certainly don't enjoy having anger directed at them. In fact, some parties use extreme emotions to coerce others, knowing that they will give in to escape the unpleasantness of the strong emotions. Anger and fear can be intense and unpleasant emotions, but emotions can be managed. How we respond to our feelings of anger and fear and how we receive others' feelings of anger will determine whether conflict is destructive or constructive.[26]

Very often, feelings are only indirectly expressed during a conflict. They leak into the conversation, not as feelings, but as other things like accusations or judgments. We hear comments such as "You set me up" or "You're inconsiderate" during a conflict. Clearly, emotions lie behind these comments, but nothing about feelings is asserted directly.

Talking directly about our feelings, saying that we feel angry, hurt, or disappointed, would be a much better way to address those feelings. However, when feelings are mentioned directly, the other person is commonly blamed for them with "you" statements, such as "You make me so angry" or "You hurt my feelings." People on the receiving end of statements like these are likely to respond defensively.

A much more effective way to talk about those feelings is to take responsibility for them, rather than blaming the other person for them, by using "I" statements

Conflict Quote ▼

It can have a profoundly negative effect on those who have to work around the explosive person. It can add to hypertension, stress-related illness.

—Eric Hollander, Professor of Psychiatry[27] ▲

instead of "you" statements. In other words, we could say something like "I feel disappointed," rather than "You let me down." One of the most effective ways to talk about feelings is to connect them to the specific behaviors of others by making statements such as "When you do *this* in *that* situation, I feel *hurt*." This approach can allow us to point out the disagreeable behavior without blaming the other person for our feelings.[28]

We also need to be aware that, like us, the other parties in a conflict can have strong feelings. When intense feelings are directed at us, it is even more difficult to manage our own emotions. So how should we respond when other people get angry? We can try to argue them out of it. We can tell them that their feelings are unreasonable or just plain stupid. But that rarely works. We're better off if we acknowledge their feelings. Of course, this is easier said than done because those feelings are likely to be expressed as accusations, judgments, and "you" statements.

Statements like "You are completely unprofessional and totally incompetent" can be difficult to listen to without becoming defensive. The key is to guide the other party away from personal attacks and toward an expression of the feelings behind the attacks. We can do this by reflecting back their feelings: "I know you're very angry right now." Or we could ask them about their feelings directly.

When other people share their feelings with us, we need to acknowledge them, but we don't have to accept responsibility for them. We need to let them know that we hear and understand their feelings, but we do not need to agree that their feelings are our fault. We may want to allow them to vent their feelings because people sometimes feel better after they've had an opportunity to air their grievances and feel like they've been listened to and understood. This is only advisable, however, if we are able to resist responding defensively or attacking them, and they are able to vent without becoming abusive.[29]

Both parties benefit from talking directly about feelings during a conflict without losing control. But as we all know, emotions can be difficult to tame. They may surge unexpectedly, be more intense than we expected, or they may hide and then resurface later. Thinking about our feelings before confronting another person can help us keep our emotions in check.[30] During a conflict, you may experience a number of interwoven feelings. Exploring them in advance of an interaction with someone else can help you understand your full range of feelings and how to handle them during the interaction.[31] Which strategies can you employ for managing your emotions during a confrontation with the other party?

- **Prepare for the emotions you and the other person will experience** before you raise an issue. Think about the feelings they will experience and how those might come out as accusations or judgments. Think ahead about how you will respond to these statements in a way that frames them as feelings about specific behaviors.
- **Detach from the immediate situation.** Sometimes when we are involved in a conflict, it seems to consume us. We can reduce our emotional involvement by reminding ourselves that time will pass. A conflict that seems very important at one point in time can seem like a very minor incident a short time later.
- **Take a time-out.** If you feel yourself losing control, you can take a time-out. You can do this by mentally counting to ten, or you can suggest a cooling down period and simply go for a walk.
- **Stay focused on your goal.** If your communication objective is to resolve a conflict constructively and maintain a good working relationship, you will need to manage your emotions well. Focusing on your goal can help you put your emotions in perspective and prevent you from saying things you will regret.

■ **Invite a third party to help.** If emotions are extreme and hostility is intense, you may need to ask a third party to facilitate or mediate any discussion. If you or the other person have become very defensive and can't see past the assignment of blame, you may require a third party to help you communicate.

NONVERBAL IMMEDIACY CUES

Much of our emotion is communicated nonverbally. The tone, pitch, and volume of our voice; our facial expressions; and even our posture communicate how we are feeling. To listen effectively during a conflict, we must use nonverbal cues to communicate our acceptance and caring for the other person.

It can be very difficult, if not downright impossible, to "lie" nonverbally. The problem is having too many things to control. If we focus on maintaining good eye contact and monitoring our facial expression, we might disclose our true feelings through a rigid body posture. Alternatively, if we truly adopt the collaborative mindset, our nonverbal communication will typically bear that out.

POSITIVE LANGUAGE

Positive and negative language both reveal and create our attitudes through the words we use. Negative language focuses on the problem rather than the solution and on limitations rather than possibilities. It has a tone of criticism and blame. Positive language, on the other hand, has an optimistic tone and focuses on what can be done. Reframing is a way of transforming negative language into positive language. Relational statements are optimistic statements about working through conflict and building a relationship. Specific behavioral statements are useful for addressing issues of blame and personal criticism. In the pages that follow, we'll examine each of these forms of positive language in a bit more detail.

REFRAMING

The way we say things, the words we use, create a "frame" that shapes our perceptions. **Reframing** is the process of creating a constructive frame or a more positive viewpoint for whatever is going on. While the objective reality may remain the same, reframing an event can change the meaning entirely. Through the reframing process, we can turn negative or hostile statements into problems to be solved collaboratively. Statements can be reframed in ways that make them more positive, future-oriented, and much more constructive. For example,[32]

■ **We can reframe personal attacks:** "You're incompetent" can be changed to "This proposal needs a little more work."

■ **We can reframe hostile statements:** "You're rude and thoughtless" becomes "I prefer to be informed of changes in advance."

■ **We can reframe statements about the past:** "For the last three weeks you haven't submitted your daily reports on time" could become a statement about the future, "We could improve operations considerably if these reports were submitted by their deadline."

■ **We can reframe criticisms:** "You're unreliable" could become a request, "Could you give me a little advance notice when you won't be able to make the meetings?"

Techniques for reframing include rephrasing, proposing an option, moving from abstract to specific, and moving from positions to interests. Some more creative ways of reframing include creating a metaphor or role-playing.

RELATIONAL STATEMENTS

Parties working through conflicts are often anxious. They may have low levels of trust in each other and be concerned that the other party will try to "win the argument." We can create a more relaxed, collaborative atmosphere by making optimistic relational statements such as, "I'm sure we can work this out." In this statement is an implicit invitation for the other party to join us in producing a solution to the conflict. Relational statements communicate that the relationship matters and we are interested in working through the issues *with* the other party to produce a mutually acceptable solution. They reduce the other party's fear that we will attack them personally, react defensively, or try to force a solution on them that is not in their best interest. Relational statements also reduce the likelihood that the other party will attack us.[34] As we work through conflict, periodically making relational statements about what is going well and noting points of agreement can contribute to the collaborative atmosphere.

SPECIFIC BEHAVIORAL STATEMENTS

It is difficult to create change in ourselves, to say nothing of creating change in others, if we're unclear about what exactly should be changed. When problem behaviors are the source of conflict, those specific behaviors should be discussed. Speaking in generalities—or worse, hurling personal criticisms—will do little to create positive change and is likely to escalate a conflict.

When we want others to change we should tell them which specific behavior is a problem for us and what we would like them to do instead. Of course, this doesn't mean they will automatically comply, but at least they'll be clear on what you want from them. Similarly, when others want us to change, if they don't offer a description of our problem behavior, we should ask for one. We can also ask them for some specific examples of what they are talking about. Again, if we hear, "You are completely unprofessional and totally incompetent," it's hard to know where to begin to improve the situation. Alternatively, if we hear, "I think it is unprofessional for you to arrive late to meetings," that's a criticism we can do something about. It helps the understanding of both parties to clarify the specific behaviors involved. This leads away from personal attacks and frames the issue as something that can be addressed.

NEGOTIATION

Negotiation is the process of working through the issues in a conflict. We often think of negotiation as something that is done by politicians, trained FBI agents, top executives, and union leaders. But in reality we all are very experienced negotiators because we do it everyday. When you work out agreements on what time to hold a meeting, or who should staff the booth at a trade show, or even where to go for lunch, you are negotiating. Negotiation is an ongoing part of relationships.

Negotiation is an active phase of conflict resolution that rests somewhere between avoiding a conflict and competing to win. It is a way of moderating conflicts that inhibits destructive behaviors, allows for self-discovery, and encourages trust between parties. During negotiation people mutually attempt to meet their goals by brainstorming ideas, generating many options, and practicing give-and-take. Even though a negotiation may seem to be only about substantive issues, the process of negotiation is really about working through the substantive issues in a way that improves the relationship between the parties.[35]

Negotiation requires that both parties engage in the process, be willing to cooperate, and use persuasive communication rather than manipulation or coercion. Solutions produced through negotiation are often packaged, meaning that a variety of alternatives is generated and the final solution is some combination of these. This works only if the negotiating parties are interdependent and have something to offer each other. Power differences can affect the ability of people to negotiate and trade off options effectively. A low-power party may seek ways to balance power, such as hiring a lawyer.[36]

Despite the potential that negotiation holds, it is often not nearly as effective as it could be. Negotiation frequently turns into positional bargaining. As you read just a few pages back, when people argue about positions instead of interests, they often lock themselves into a position and make it sound as if only one solution would be acceptable. This effect is worsened in negotiation by the fact that people tend to make the first statements of their position more extreme, since they expect to make some concessions. ("I'm willing to pay $200,000, but I'll offer $150,000 to start.") Interests that may be compatible or even shared may not be revealed through arguing positions. In negotiation, arguing over positions is bad for the process and makes satisfying agreement less likely.[37]

Conflict Quote ▼

It's common for negotiators to confuse the deal and the relationship. They feel that if they push too hard to get the best deal possible today, they may jeopardize their company's ability to do business with the other party in the future. Or they fear that if they pay too much attention to the relationship, they'll end up giving away too much and make a lousy deal.

—Danny Ertel, Founding Partner of Vantage Partners LLC[38] ▲

People can have different approaches to the negotiation process, ranging from competitive to collaborative approaches. During the process, people may swing from competitive to collaborative and across all points in between, often beginning with a competitive approach that accomplishes little but soon realizing the advantage of using a collaborative approach.[39]

COMPETITIVE APPROACHES

Competitive approaches are based on the assumption that resources are limited or that the size of the "pie" is fixed and that the only acceptable strategy is a win/lose mindset, where each party tries to get the largest slice of the pie for themselves. Communication patterns of the competitive style include threats, confrontation, and argumentation. Information is often concealed or is misleading. Competitive tactics include opening with high demands and making small and slow concessions that are timed for maximum effect, and then exaggerating their value.[40]

Competitive approaches have several distinct disadvantages. They tend to be shortsighted, based on the assumption that one negotiation will not have an effect on later relations, but, of course, it can. Confrontational and coercive techniques can damage relationships, breeding mistrust, anger, resentment, and hostility. Competitive approaches, since they undermine trust and relationships, inhibit the open sharing of information necessary to achieve joint gains. So this approach produces the sort of exchange that prevents the development of collaborative solutions that satisfy both parties.[41]

COLLABORATIVE APPROACHES

Collaborative approaches, by contrast, attempt to find integrative solutions that produce maximum joint gains. In some cases, integrative solutions are easy to produce, such as when parties want opposite things that don't cancel each other out. A classic fable illustrates this. Two sisters were arguing over a single orange. Finally, they agreed to split the orange in half. This compromise left them each dissatisfied with the solution, since they each wanted an entire orange—one for the juice and one for the peel to use in a cake. If they had simply shared their interests instead of arguing their positions or wanting the entire orange, they could have produced an integrative solution that maximized their joint rewards.[42]

Collaborative approaches to negotiation assume that sharing information about interests will allow parties to expand the "pie" by finding things that can be exchanged to create a solution package. In labor negotiations, conflicts over wages are often settled with a solution package that includes more than just pay. Collaborative communication strategies often involve an effort to find things—other than the central content of the conflict—that can be exchanged to create a solution package. People may

- **logroll,** so that all parties disclose multiple important interests and make trades so that each gets the one that is most important to them;
- **cost cut,** which seeks to minimize the cost to the other party of going along with a solution; and
- **bridge,** where parties try to invent new options to meet the other party's needs.[43]

Communication patterns of collaborative approaches reveal optimism that a solution exists, a willingness to work at generating many solutions, a concern for the relationship, and a concern that the outcome meets some sort of standard for a good solution. Here are some examples of phrases that might be used in collaborative communication.

Phrases that communicate a *concern for the relationship:*

- This relationship is important to me.
- We've gotten through other difficult moments and we'll get through this.
- I know we can find a solution that works for both of us.
- We're going to work this out.

Phrases that communicate *a willingness to explore interests:*

- What would you like to see happen?
- What concerns you most?
- If things turned out this way, how would you feel about that?

Phrases that note *areas of common interest:*

- We both want. . . .
- We both agree that. . . .
- We have the same ultimate goal.
- We want the same thing; we just want to go about getting it differently.

People frequently produce a suboptimal solution when they negotiate, though. Fisher, Ury, and Patton, authors of *Getting to Yes,* suggest that one main reason for this is the tendency for people to make premature judgments. Judging ideas during the production phase simply inhibits idea generation. If people feel they are being judged, they can be reluctant to put forth suggestions. As with brainstorming, it can be advantageous to separate the process of inventing options from the process of evaluating them.

The process of generating many, varied ideas also can be stunted by the notion that there is just one *best* idea or one true solution. Another way to encourage people to suggest options freely is to purposely offer alternatives you know are impractical or suggest two alternatives at the same time. Either of these techniques demonstrates to the other person a willingness to discuss many options and that suggesting an alternative does not mean commitment to that alternative.[44]

Before beginning the negotiation process, it can be helpful to lay some ground rules. In general, rules should be designed to keep the negotiation on track and prevent parties from engaging in personal attacks or showing disrespect. Rules might include things such as "no personal insults allowed," "only one person talks at a time," or "when one person talks, the other person agrees to listen." In some cases, you may want to take the pressure off the session by agreeing *not* to come to a final agreement at that particular meeting.

"DIRTY TRICKS"

During a negotiation, people may refuse to cooperate or may resort to what Fisher, Ury, and Patton call "dirty tricks."[45] Common dirty tricks include lying about facts. An entrepreneur named Sarah was looking for a retail space to open a small shop. A realty broker representing a mall owner quoted the lease rate to her for an open space in the mall. Sarah went to look at the space and decided she wanted it, but when she went to negotiate the lease with the owner, he quoted her a price higher than what the realty broker had given. Sarah asked about the discrepancy and the owner replied, "Oh I told her that price two years ago when she first started working with me. I can show you the paperwork with the dates on it." Of course, Sarah could understand how the rate could increase over two years. Still, she contacted the broker to let her know what happened. When Sarah relayed what the owner had said, the broker replied that she had confirmed the price with him right before she told Sarah the rates. When Sarah discovered the mall owner's dirty trick, she resumed her search for space.

Dirty tricks can include other forms of deception, such as people presenting themselves as having the authority to make an agreement when they really don't or people misrepresenting their intention to comply with whatever agreement is made. Other tactics include methods of making the negotiation unpleasant so that other people are motivated to end the process early, even if it means making an agreement that isn't in their best interest. This can be accomplished by subtly communicating personal attacks, such as "You don't look like you're feeling well" or "Surely you must realize . . ." (implying that you are ignorant if you don't). People may try to make others feel as if they are not important by making them wait, taking phone calls during the negotiation, or allowing for other interruptions. Threats are also a commonly used tactic. Threats can be particularly damaging to relationships and may backfire by complicating the process of coming to an agreement for some who feel that giving in to threats will cause them to lose face.[46]

When the other party in a negotiation refuses to negotiate or uses a competitive approach, you can attempt to pull that person into collaboration by staying focused on interests and not reacting to personal attacks. When attacked, try not to attack back. If your ideas are attacked, try not to defend them. Instead, look beyond the attacks and the positions to identify the *interests* of the other party. Try to reframe an attack on you as an attack on the problem.[47]

EVALUATING SOLUTIONS

Even when both parties decide to cooperate, it is possible that an acceptable agreement may not be reached. How do you protect yourself from accepting an agreement that you really should reject? Typically, people at least want to know their bottom line in a negotiation. The bottom line is the worst acceptable outcome to the negotiation. You want to pay $2,000 in rent per month for your office. You may refuse to pay more than $2,500, so $2,500 is your bottom line.

Focusing on the bottom line protects you from making an unwise agreement. But it can also inhibit the production of creative alternatives. Maybe paying $2,500 would be okay if the utilities or certain maintenance costs were included in that amount. In some cases, being too focused on the bottom line will prevent you from accepting an agreement you really should take. You may not want to pay more than $2,500, but what if space in the area you desire is scarce? You may refuse a rate of $2,600 because it is beyond your bottom line, but you may find no other alternatives available in your desired location.

Fisher, Ury, and Patton recommend knowing your *best alternative to the negotiated agreement,* or BATNA. Your BATNA is different from your bottom line. While your bottom line is the worst acceptable outcome of the negotiation, your BATNA is the best alternative you will have if the negotiation falls through. Instead of focusing on the bottom line, parties using their BATNA ask themselves about the best alternative for them if they fail to reach an agreement. Using a BATNA as a way of deciding whether to accept an agreement protects you from walking away from a less-than-perfect agreement to an even worse alternative.[48]

To prepare for a negotiation, you should work to develop a clear sense of your BATNA. If you know your alternative to the negotiated agreement and it isn't all that bad, then you're less likely to agree to something that really isn't in your best interest. The better your BATNA, the more power you have in the negotiation.[49]

What other techniques can you use to evaluate an agreement? To ensure that the agreement you're accepting will work for you *and* the other party, you should compare it with objective criteria you've agreed upon in advance.[50] For example, managers and clerical workers may have different interests when it comes to scheduling breaks and vacations. A criterion for a good solution for management might be that only a certain number of clerical workers be away from the office at a time. For the clerical workers, a criterion might be that breaks occur at the same time each day. Whatever schedule is produced in negotiation would be compared with the criteria before being accepted.

Setting standards can lead to a wiser and fairer solution. However, agreeing on criteria can in itself require some negotiation. You can begin by agreeing on generalities rather than specifics. For example, you may agree that you want to set a fair price, create a just rule, produce a quality product, write a workable policy, or simply be able to work together. After reaching this initial agreement, the search for specific criteria can begin. Often, objective standards such as market value, scientific findings, or cost/benefit ratios can be used. Remember that if you suggest a requirement, you should be prepared to explain your reasons for wanting it included. The criteria should reflect the interests of both parties.[51]

MEDIATION

What can managers do when the conflict to resolve is not their own, but that of their employees? Managers faced with employee conflict can ignore it, separate the employees, terminate one or both of the employees, send them to counseling, hire a third party to intervene or intervene themselves.[52] The goal of third-party intervention is to assist in transforming the conflict elements in some way. A manager can use a number of approaches to accomplish this general goal. Managers can alter the degree of interdependence between the parties, change perceptions of goals so they are not seen as incompatible, increase a resource to reduce competition due to scarcity, or alter the perceived or actual interference of one party with the other's goal attainment. Or managers can mediate conflicts.

Managers can act as mediators or facilitators of employee conflicts that require intervention if they are able to remain neutral and if they are of a higher status than the conflicting parties. The goals of **mediation** range from facilitating organizational change to facilitating dialogue to breaking destructive cycles to reaching an agreement in principle to reaching a written agreement.[53] Mediation should not be used to establish guilt or innocence, to discipline or punish, or to decide right and wrong. It is not an appropriate approach to deal with violations of a legal or

Conflict Quote ▼

Christopher Komisarjevsky is chairman and chief executive of Burson-Marsteller, a global public relations firm. His strategy is to let employees work out their own conflicts. "Every organization has an inherent level of conflict within it," he says. "That's actually a form of competition that's healthy. In tough times, though, some people will begin to react politically rather than professionally," and it can have a devastating effect on an organization.

"Most organizations today are made up of teams," says Komisarjevsky. But "numerous times when people are thrown together, they don't like each other or don't agree with each other." When that happens, he says, managers have a few choices: They can fire one person or another. They can fire all of them. Or, they can put them in a room together and say, "Work it out or I expect your resignations." Usually, they work it out.

"I have a great overriding confidence in human beings and in their intelligence and ability to find a solution if there is an overriding goal." You really need to anticipate conflict when very talented individuals work together, but they need to recognize that "at the end of the day, it's the success of the team that matters."[54] ▲

ethical code. Nor is it an appropriate strategy for dealing with personal problems, such as performance issues caused by substance abuse.[55]

Mediation, while involving a third party, still leaves the production of a solution largely to the conflicting parties. This is a particular advantage of mediation. Solutions produced in this way are more likely to be integrative since both parties are involved in creating them and are more likely to be followed because each party will have a stake in them.[56] However, because both parties must participate in formulating the solution, mediation is only effective when they are willing and able to do so. Mediation isn't a good choice if people seriously mistrust each other, largely because they will not communicate openly. It also doesn't work if the relationship is weak or perceived as unimportant because the people involved won't be motivated to participate in this sometimes arduous process. Mediation also may not be a good choice if people are extremely antagonistic because they must be able to suspend hostilities and refrain from threats for the mediation meeting.[57]

Rather than solving the conflict for the people involved, mediators primarily serve as listeners and guides for the resolution process. Mediators structure and guide sessions, encourage people to see things from a variety of viewpoints, stimulate the discussion, and educate people about the process. They may ask questions to help those involved explore each other's perspectives and reframe comments in a more positive way. In some cases, they will offer suggestions, and in most cases, they will formulate, in written form, the final collaborative agreement.[58]

MANAGERS AS MEDIATORS

To act as a mediator for an employee dispute, managers should begin the process by holding preliminary meetings with each of the parties in private, just to hear each side of the story. The goal of the manager is not to judge or to take sides but to hear and understand the various views. After hearing the parties' sides, the manager then determines what problem must be solved. This allows the manager to focus the mediation on the business problem at hand and on creating a successful working relationship between the parties, rather than allowing the parties to focus the mediation on things they don't like about each other. At the preliminary meeting, managers can also describe the purpose of the mediation, explain the rules of the mediation meeting (e.g., listen respectfully, take turns speaking), and ensure the parties' willingness to participate.[59]

To prepare for a mediation meeting, the manager should attend to the environmental and psychological elements that will affect just how useful the meeting will be. The location should be neutral, private, and free from interruptions and distractions. Seating arrangements and other aspects of the physical surroundings should also be considered, as should the time of day, day of the week, and time allotted for the meeting. Since the people involved may represent other constituents, the manager may also want to consider who else should be present at the meeting.[60]

At a mediation meeting, the manager should work to create a constructive and positive atmosphere and set the expectations for each step of the mediation. The mediating manager should regulate the discussion by determining the sequence for speaking; monitoring the discussion for sincerity, openness, and understanding; and help the parties involved get back on track if they start to deviate from the process. The manager must watch for rule violations in the meetings, such as personal attacks, and point them out as violations. Managers may call for a timeout to relieve tension if the discussion becomes too heated.[61] The manager can also contribute to a positive atmosphere by noting conciliatory gestures that may otherwise go unnoticed. In most cases, but not all, mediation managers should refrain from giving advice, offering solutions, or stating opinions.[62]

As a mediation meeting comes to a close, the solution proposal, if one has been produced, should be examined to see if it is balanced, behaviorally specific, and measurable. The manager's task then is to record the solution and distribute copies to the parties involved. It is also the manager's responsibility to follow up with everyone to ensure that the solution agreed to is actually implemented.[63]

PROFESSIONAL MEDIATION

Professional mediators will be a better choice than a manager mediator when the conflict is very complex or when the manager doubts her ability to handle mediation or to remain impartial. Professional mediators come from a variety of backgrounds and bring with them a variety of styles and goals for mediation. Some mediators may simply be concerned with reaching a settlement, while others may see the mediation as an opportunity to create change and transform relationships. Mediators with legal backgrounds tend to be more focused on content issues and attend less to relationship issues. Mediators with higher status, such as those with a known reputation, may use reflexive, distributive, or representation techniques (asking one side to state the other's position) because the parties are more likely to listen to a higher-status mediator. Techniques such as threatening, rewarding, information gathering, empowering, and agenda setting can also be employed with a higher-status mediator. However, mediators who examine relationship, identity, and process issues typically produce better solutions.[64]

Some professional mediators use strategies that require minimal amounts of information and consider few alternatives in order to save time. Quick solutions may sound tempting, but they are less likely to address the personal issues that emotionally charge the conflict.[65] Mediators who are most effective at achieving a satisfying agreement attempt to improve the relationship between the disputants, rather than just push for settlement or focus on facts. They tend to be

- impartial,
- empathic,
- skilled at communication,
- good at asking questions, and
- knowledgeable about many different problem-solving techniques.

While professional mediations will vary by issue and mediator, some generalities apply. A professional mediation typically begins with the mediator's introductory remarks. This is an opportunity for the mediator to describe his or her role, outline the process, define the time frame, set the ground rules, and summarize the problem as it has been stated in any briefs submitted before the meeting. The parties will then each have an opportunity to explain the problem according to their perspective. The mediator will then ask the parties open-ended questions to take the exploration of the problem further, attempt to find common ground or goals between the parties, and identify which issues will be settled during the meeting. In this "storytelling" phase of the mediation, problems are discussed in terms of fears, concerns, and interests. In this phase, venting sometimes occurs, and mediators are on guard for that, defusing such behavior when it threatens to derail the process. Mediators also ask questions that probe for interests, such as "What will it take for you to agree?" or "How would you like to be treated?"[66]

Sometimes barriers occur in the mediation process and the most reasonable approach is to call a caucus. A **caucus** is a private meeting between a party and the mediator. Any party or the mediator can call for a caucus at any time. A caucus can be used to reduce tension between parties, clarify interests, explain the costs of no settlement, and so on. If a caucus will take some

Conflict Quote ▼

The advantage of mediation is that a skillful mediator can often find a common ground for resolution that the parties otherwise fail to recognize.

—Robert Fitzpatrick, Esq., Fitzpatrick & Associates[67] ▲

time, a formal break should be called so the other party isn't kept waiting. And when the meeting resumes, the mediator should explain the purpose and results of the caucus to the other party, although no information from the caucus should be shared unless the party involved in the caucus agrees.[68]

Participants should agree on the criteria for evaluating ideas, and the ideas produced by the discussion should be checked against them. When participants reach a solution, the parties involved should draft a *memorandum of understanding* that summarizes their agreement. The mediator is responsible for writing the final agreement. That final document should mention each of the parties by name and scrupulously avoid any mention of blame. It should also be very specific in its description of who will do what, when, how, and where in order to fulfill the agreement. It should, additionally, explain any penalties for failing to fulfill terms of the agreement. Such documents don't serve any legally binding purpose but do create a common memory of the agreement and expectations of what will happen next for each of the parties.[69]

Not all mediations produce a settlement. Agreements are more likely when conflicts have not escalated to a heated level. At the same time, mediation is ineffective if the conflict is so new that disputants have suffered very few negative consequences from the disagreement. In that case, the motivation of the parties to participate in mediation may be low. People are usually satisfied with the mediation process because it is faster, cheaper, and more enduring than other forms of conflict resolution. The agreements are more satisfying and more likely to be followed because they are tailored to the disputants' needs.[70]

FACILITATION

Facilitation is similar to mediation in that a third party has the role of assisting the conflicting parties in the conflict resolution process. Facilitation is more commonly used when larger groups, experiencing moderate levels of conflict, are involved. It often takes place in a public context, and people who have expertise in the area of concern are invited to participate in the discussion. Not all group situations are right for facilitation, though. It is most useful when the problems the groups face are complex and not better solved with a unilateral decision. The groups involved must be able to tolerate being in the same space with each other, so it is a better choice when the groups are not polarized to the point of being completely hostile.[71]

It is the facilitator's job to create an environment that promotes participation in the discussion, to regulate the discussion, and to provide the tools—including procedures—necessary for the communication process. When it's done well, facilitation can also help build or improve the relationship between groups. Managers, though, can serve as facilitators only if both groups see them as sufficiently neutral.[72]

As with mediation, environmental or contextual concerns for the meeting, such as the day of the week, time of day, amount of time allotted for the process, size of the room, and seating arrangements should be considered. During the meeting, the role of the facilitator is to help the groups determine the goals for the meeting and to lay ground rules for participation. The rules for groups must accomplish the goals of creating a safe environment for communication, limiting the participation of those who would dominate the conversation and encouraging the more passive participants.[73]

During the meeting, a facilitator helps the groups involved use effective communication tools for reaching their objectives. Providing them with a good set of procedures can protect their meeting from the most common complaints about group meetings: people getting off topic, one person dominating, a few people not participating, and people being unclear about the goals of the meeting. As the meeting progresses, a facilitator can periodically summarize the points the groups have made and clarify any misunderstandings. Facilitators can also help groups see their commonalities by pointing out when those groups agree on something. They can protect the communication environment by reframing toxic comments and by making observations that get the groups to recognize how they are talking about things.[74]

Facilitators, though, are only as effective as the meeting management tools and techniques they possess. Managers can easily learn to use many of the more common facilitation techniques, including:

- **Problem census.** This is a technique for identifying a problem where each person at the meeting is asked to present one problem until all problems have been identified, then the people vote on the items they think are most important.
- **Brainstorming.** This is the classic technique for producing ideas, where ideas are generated and not evaluated in the first phase, and then the ideas with the most merit are identified and discussed in the second phase.
- **Nominal group technique.** The nominal group technique requires members to write down ideas individually, then the ideas are discussed and clarified, and each group ranks the ideas in order of importance.
- **The talking circle.** In the talking circle, four chairs are placed in the middle of the group and only those who sit in the chairs are allowed to participate in the discussion. Observers must take the place of a member of the circle to join the discussion. Discussion does not occur between the observers and the circle, but a member of the circle can call for an observer to become part of the circle.
- **Risk technique.** Evaluating a solution can be done with the risk technique, which asks people to give their thoughts on the risks of a solution that has been produced. After the meeting, a list of concerns is sent to everyone. Those lists are then returned to the facilitator with additional concerns added and the original concerns refined. That feedback is distributed and is used as the subject of the next meeting.
- **Parking lot.** In order to keep groups from getting far off the immediate topics, facilitators can record tangential issues that come up during the discussion on a white board or flip chart designated as the "parking lot." Those issues can then be discussed later when they won't detract attention from the immediate topic.

In addition to using these tools effectively, succeeding as a facilitator can take a little practice. Group dynamics have a way of sucking unsuspecting facilitators into traps that impede any progress for the groups. Facilitators can lose control of the process if the group gets off on tangential matters, and—as a result—they may feel pressure to produce a solution and may try to get there too quickly. The groups may also begin talking about something that they have no power over, a third group, which the groups see as victimizing both of them.[75]

Facilitation with large groups is not likely to produce a solution with which everyone completely agrees. But solutions can be accepted with varying levels of agreement among individuals in the groups. At the end of the meeting, whether the issues have been resolved or not, the facilitator must help the groups find closure by summarizing the progress, clarifying agreements, helping the group agree on the next step, and making sure the group gets a summary of the meeting.[76]

OTHER METHODS OF INTERVENTION

ARBITRATION

In **arbitration,** the conflicting parties have a role in sharing information, but the solution is actually produced by the third party and may be binding, whether the conflicting parties like the solution or not. Conflicting parties turn to arbitration because they mutually agree to empower a third party to settle their dispute, or because they are ordered to do so by a judge, or compelled to do so by a contract. Both sides get to argue their case in front of the arbitrator that the parties select, often from a list of qualified arbitrators supplied by the American Arbitration Association.[77]

Conflict Quote ▼

The decision to seek arbitration is sometimes made after a conflict has arisen, but much more often the parties have a clause in their contract committing them to arbitration of disputes arising from their business together.
—John Allison, Professor of Business, University of Texas[78] ▲

Before a meeting, documents may be submitted to the arbitrator for review and sometimes a pre-hearing is held. During the actual hearing, the arbitrator may ask clarifying questions. Decisions are typically made within 30 days of the hearing and no explanation of the decision is required.[79] In a binding arbitration, both parties contractually agree to follow the ruling of the arbitrator. Voluntary arbitration allows for further arbitration or a court battle if one or both parties do not accept the judgment of the arbitrator. In many cases, the arbitrator is an expert in the area of the dispute and may be able to produce solutions that the parties could not come up with on their own.[80]

Arbitration offers the advantage of putting the process of conflict resolution in motion so that parties cannot simply reach an impasse. Cases may wind up in arbitration because parties do not care enough about the relationship to cooperate. Arbitration is useful when issues are clear-cut, but parties are deadlocked. Arbitration addresses only content issues, however, and not relational aspects of a conflict.[81] In for-profit business organizations, this option is probably not best in most cases, and managers should be wary of conflicting parties who ask for binding arbitration. It tends to promote the idea that escalating conflicts, while not learning how to resolve them, is a legitimate strategy for dealing with conflict because, ultimately, they get resolved through arbitration.[82]

ADJUDICATION

The legal system takes over when it is assumed that the parties cannot reach an agreement by themselves. With **adjudication,** decisions are made by a judge or jury after the legal representatives of the parties argue their clients' positions. In some cases, the legal representatives may negotiate a resolution before appearing before the court. The parties, thus, do not participate in producing a solution, but the solution is ultimately binding.[83]

The disadvantages of adjudication are well known and many. First and foremost, it can be expensive. Around $20 billion a year is spent on lawyers' fees in the United States.[84] The parties in conflict are removed from the process of producing solutions, and frequently a solution is produced that neither party finds satisfying. Legal representatives will take a competitive approach to solving the problem and may escalate the conflict and damage the relationship between parties as they attempt to get the best deal they can. Finally, the system is overused and often abused, in part because lawyers, whose fees are based on a percentage of an award, are motivated to bring as many suits as possible.[85]

Adjudication can offer some advantages in certain cases. It sets in motion a process that cannot be ignored by the other party. If a complaint is filed, avoidance becomes a nonoption. In the United States, all citizens are constitutionally guaranteed equal protection under the law, so parties of low power can use the law to level the playing field. The process also strives to be fair, assuming advocates of approximately equal skill. Both sides get an opportunity to speak, admit evidence, and have their cases prepared and argued by trained legal experts.[87]

> **Conflict Quote ▼**
>
> *For well over a decade the American workplace has been a veritable war zone. Disgruntled employees and their creative lawyers file countless claims against employers. The only consistent winners in this war have been the lawyers.*
>
> —Robert Fitzpatrick, Esq., Fitzpatrick & Associates[86] ▲

CONCLUSION

Conflict is inevitable, even in the best of business relationships. And it's increasingly likely as the workforce continues to become more diverse. But that's not necessarily a bad thing. As we've seen, organizational outcomes can be improved with a certain amount of conflict, and at a personal level, professional relationships can be strengthened. The beneficial or detrimental effects of conflict depend on how it's handled.

We've discussed that for working relationships, where patterns of interaction are established, a conflict can be viewed as an episode in an ongoing communication process. To understand any conflict fully and determine the best way to resolve it, we must look at the entire conflict system. We may determine that a conflict can be solved by increasing a resource or by making a minor procedural change. Alternatively, we may decide that the best, most effective way to deal with a conflict is to confront the other party.

Confrontation doesn't guarantee a successful resolution. We've seen that, when mishandled, confrontation may escalate conflict. Working through a conflict to produce a solution that both parties will be happy with and, at the same time, strengthen the relationship between the parties, requires collaborative communication and dialogue. We can achieve this communication goal by adopting a collaborative mindset, listening effectively, and using positive language. Even when we are acting as a third party to employee conflicts or have employed a professional to intervene, the goal should be the same: collaborative communication.

Managing conflict in a constructive fashion means dealing with disagreement or differing viewpoints in ways that respect the individuals involved. The process of working through conflict constructively can strengthen the relationship between parties by allowing them the opportunity to demonstrate this respect, despite adverse circumstances. The most useful long-term by-product of that process will be shared trust.

Working through conflict constructively also allows us to learn about ourselves as we learn about each other by encouraging us to understand our own perspectives, emotions, and goals. No matter where we encounter conflict—at work, at home, or in a social setting—our message is simple: The techniques discussed in this book can help each of us learn to better manage conflict in ways that promote self-knowledge and build stronger, more functional, more productive relationships.

DISCUSSION QUESTIONS

1. Discuss how communication shapes conflicts.

2. How does dialogue compare with the communication typically used in conflicts?

3. During a conflict it is important to control emotions, yet not ignore feelings. Discuss the difference between controlling emotions and ignoring feelings. Why are emotions so important in conflict?

4. Is it ever advisable to use dirty tricks in a negotiation? When and why?

5. When you plan a negotiation meeting, one thing you will need to consider is the seating arrangement. Should you and the other party sit facing each other, side-by-side, or at a ninety-degree angle along the corner of the table? What difference does it make?

6. Is it best to know your BATNA and your bottom line? What is the difference between these two? Is one more useful than the other?

7. Under what circumstances would you call in a professional third party to help with a conflict? What would indicate to you that this step was necessary?

ENDNOTES
1. William W. Wilmot and Joyce L. Hocker, *Interpersonal Conflict,* 6th ed. (New York: McGraw-Hill, 2001).
2. Wilmot and Hocker.
3. Ibid.
4. Ibid.
5. Ibid.
6. William C. Taylor, "The Leader of the Future," *Fast Company,* vol. 25, June 1999. Available: http://www.fastcompany.com/online/25/heifetz.html.

7. Cheryl Dahle, "Don't Get Mad—Get over It," *Fast Company,* vol. 22, February 1999. Available: http://www.fastcompany.com/online/22/toolbox.html.
8. Roger Fisher and Scott Brown, *Getting Together: Building Relationships as We Negotiate* (New York: Penguin Books, 1988).
9. Wilmot and Hocker.
10. Fisher and Brown.
11. Stephen W. Littlejohn and Kathy Domenici, *Engaging Communication in Conflict* (Thousand Oaks, CA: Sage, 2001).
12. Fisher and Brown.
13. James J. Floyd, *Listening: A Practical Approach* (Glenview, IL: Scott, Foresman, 1982).
14. Littlejohn and Domenici.
15. Douglas Stone, Bruce Patton, and Sheila Heen, *Difficult Conversations* (New York: Viking Press, 1999).
16. Littlejohn and Domenici.
17. Robert Bacal, "Organizational Conflict: The Good, the Bad, and the Ugly." Available: http://www.work911.com/ articles/orgconflict.htm.
18. Roger Fisher, William Ury, and Bruce Patton, *Getting to Yes: Negotiating Agreement without Giving In,* 2nd ed. (New York: Penguin Books, 1991).
19. Fisher, Ury, and Patton.
20. Wilmot and Hocker.
21. Stone, Patton, and Heen.
22. Fisher, Ury, and Patton.
23. Taylor.
24. Stone, Patton, and Heen.
25. Fisher, Ury, and Patton.
26. Wilmot and Hocker.
27. Beth Nissen, "Overworked, Overwrought: 'Desk Rage' at Work," November 15, 2000. Available: http://www.cnn.com.
28. J. C. Gottman, J. Gonso Notarius, and H. Markman, *A Couple's Guide to Communication* (Champaign, IL: Research Press, 1976).
29. Fisher, Ury, and Patton.
30. Fisher and Brown.
31. Stone, Patton, and Heen.
32. Littlejohn and Domenici.
33. Erik J. Van Slyke, *Listening to Conflict: Finding Constructive Solutions to Workplace Disputes* (New York: Amacon, 1999), 85.
34. Fisher and Brown.
35. Wilmot and Hocker.
36. Ibid.
37. Fisher, Ury, and Patton.
38. Danny Ertel, "Turning Negotiation into a Corporate Capability," *Harvard Business Review on Negotiation and Conflict Resolution* (Boston: Harvard Business School Press, 2000), 113.
39. Wilmot and Hocker.
40. Ibid.
41. Ibid.
42. M. P. Follet, *The Collected Papers of M. P. Follet,* edited by H. C. Metcalf and L. Urwick (New York: Harper and Brothers, 1940).
43. Wilmot and Hocker.
44. Fisher, Ury, and Patton.
45. Ibid.

46. Ibid.
47. Ibid.
48. Ibid.
49. Ibid.
50. Ibid.
51. Ibid.
52. Daniel Dana, *Conflict Resolution* (New York: McGraw-Hill, 2001).
53. Myra W. Isenhart and Michael Spangle, *Collaborative Approaches to Resolving Conflict* (Thousand Oaks, CA: Sage, 2000).
54. Christopher Komisarjevsky, telephone interview, New York, NY, February 28, 2003.
55. Dana.
56. Wilmot and Hocker.
57. Isenhart and Spangle.
58. Ibid.
59. Dana.
60. Ibid.
61. Robert R. Blake and Jane S. Mouton, "Overcoming Group Warfare," *Harvard Business Review on Negotiation and Conflict Resolution* (Boston: Harvard Business School Press, 2000).
62. Dana.
63. Ibid.
64. Wilmot and Hocker.
65. James A. Wall, John B. Strak, and Rhetta L. Standifer, "Mediation: A Current Review and Theory Development," *Journal of Conflict Resolution,* 4 (2001): 370–391.
66. Isenhart and Spangle.
67. Robert B. Fitapatrick, "The War in the Workplace Must End, but Arbitration is Not the Answer," *SHRM Legal Report,* Spring 1994. Available: http://www.shrm.org.
68. Isenhart and Spangle.
69. Ibid.
70. Wall, Strak, and Standifer.
71. Isenhart and Spangle.
72. Ibid.
73. Ibid.
74. Ibid.
75. Ibid.
76. Ibid.
77. Ibid.
78. John R. Allison, "Five Ways to Keep Disputes Out of Court," *Harvard Business Review on Negotiation and Conflict Resolution* (Boston: Harvard Business School Press, 2000).
79. Isenhart and Spangle.
80. Ibid.
81. Ibid.
82. Wilmot and Hocker.
83. Ibid.
84. Allison.
85. Wilmot and Hocker.
86. Fitzpatrick.
87. Wilmot and Hocker.

A CASES

CHICAGO'S MUSEUM OF CONTEMPORARY ART: BITING THE HAND THAT FEEDS IT

In recent years, museums have moved from the twilight to the spotlight of public attention. This shift is reflected not only in an increase in the number of museums but in the dramatic growth of their audience. Directing and managing a great museum is at once singularly privileged and peculiarly demanding. In a learned institution thickly populated with individualists, scholars, experts, and not a few eccentrics, gaining clarity of purpose can be difficult, especially in areas concerned with serving the public.

Museums in effect serve two client groups: their collections, and the public, who as enquirers, scholars, students, or general visitors, demand and deserve access to those collections. There is an inescapable tension in all museums between satisfying the needs of today and protecting the interests of tomorrow—between access and conservation. There are fundamental issues that need to be addressed about museum funding and management, but the debate lies dead in the water, awash in a sea of unchallenged assumptions.[1]

WHAT IS ART?

The *Oxford American Dictionary* defines art as (1) works such as paintings or sculptures produced by skill; (2) the production of something beautiful, skill or ability in such work; (3) any practical skill or knack, such as the art of sailing.

Chicago's Museum of Contemporary Art (MCA) exemplifies art on all three levels. First and foremost, the MCA's permanent collection features some of the most important artwork in the last fifty years. Many of its temporary exhibits have achieved international acclaim for daring and relevance. Also, the museum is committed to introducing and exposing the work of younger, more experimental artists to a broader and more diverse audience. Second and equally important, the MCA is committed to its role as educator.

Each year, the museum invites more than 15,000 Chicago school children, as well as community groups, to visit, tour, and learn about the museum in general and modern art in particular. The MCA works with local colleges to help improve those schools' fine arts curricula. Workshops, lectures, symposia, and informal talks by artists and curators are just some of the channels through which learning can take place at the museum. Through exposure, the MCA hopes to increase the appreciation, if not the understanding, of modern art.

Finally, the MCA believes in the "art of a deal." Thus, it is not surprising that the MCA found itself on the front page of the Marketplace section of *The Wall Street Journal* on January 13, 1998. Actually, the nature of its appearance sent shockwaves throughout the worldwide museum community. Why? The answer is because the *Journal* was reporting on the art of a deal gone wrong. The MCA became the first museum ever to sue donors over an unhonored pledge. It may be cliché, but nothing says modern more than a lawsuit. How contemporary, indeed.

THE HISTORY OF THE MCA

In October 1967, a group of culturally concerned Chicagoans, recognizing the need for an internationally oriented forum for contemporary art in their city, opened the Museum of Contemporary Art in a one-story building in the heart of the downtown. From its premiere exhibit, *Pictures to Be Read/Poetry to Be Seen,* to performance artist Chris Brown lying under a sheet of glass for 45 hours, the MCA, during its first ten years, earned an international reputation for presenting groundbreaking exhibitions of work by local, national, and international artists.

In 1979, the MCA expanded into an adjacent townhouse, more than tripling its exhibition space. With tremendously popular shows such as the Robert Maplethorpe and the Franz Kline exhibitions in the years that followed, the MCA Board of Trustees commissioned an independent study in 1985 to gauge the museum's prospects for growth. The study confirmed the critical need for a larger facility. In 1989, a campaign goal of $55 million was established to build and operate the new facility.

In 1990, Paul Oliver-Hoffmann, a real estate developer and the sitting MCA Chairman of the Board, pledged $5 million toward the campaign goal. His pledge served to attract other generous donations. The MCA also relied on this pledge when it sought $50 million worth of commercial financing to begin construction of the new facility.

Groundbreaking took place in late 1993, and the new MCA opened in July 1996. With almost seven times the square footage of the museum's previous facility, the MCA, for the first time in its history, could display its permanent collection and mount temporary exhibitions simultaneously. The MCA's first major show in its new home, *Art in Chicago: 1945–1995,* opened to public and critical acclaim.

FUNDING OF THE MCA

The Museum of Contemporary Art is a nonprofit, tax-exempt organization. The MCA's exhibitions, programming, and operations are member-supported and privately funded through contributions from individuals, corporations, and foundations. Additional support is provided through the Illinois Arts Council, a state agency, and a City Arts 4 Grant from the City of Chicago Department of Cultural Affairs. Of all the art museums in Chicago, however, the MCA receives the lowest amount of city and state funds.

In 1997, the museum had more than 16,000 members, each paying anywhere from $30 to $315 for one- or two-year memberships. Oprah Winfrey, a nationally syndicated talk show host who lives nearby, is just one of the many individuals to extend financial support. Molex, Inc., a global electronic components company, is one of the many corporations that fund various museum undertakings. (Molex funding helped cover the cost of designing and maintaining the MCA's web site: http://www.mcachicago.org.) The Lila Wallace–Reader's Digest Fund is one of the more prominent foundations that support the MCA's activities. A grant from this foundation has helped the MCA achieve its goal of developing marketing strategies and educational programs that specifically target the college-age audience.

General admission is $10 for adults and $6 for students and senior citizens. Admission is free for MCA members, for children 12 and under, and for all on Tuesdays from 5 to 8 p.m. Annual attendance averages around 375,000. The museum employs ninety full-time workers and hundreds of volunteers. The museum's restaurant, M Café, just covers its costs, while the gift shop, like those in most museums, is a healthy profit center. In fact, it's not unusual for a gift shop to provide 20 to 40 percent of a museum or exhibition's operating revenues.[2] The 1996–1997 annual budget for the MCA was $12.8 million.

POWER FEUD AT THE MCA

Paul Oliver-Hoffmann was invited onto the MCA Board of Trustees in 1981. With the invitation to sit on the board came a request for a contribution of $10,000. In fact, four basic commitments are expected of board members. They must attend board meetings, serve on at least one committee, attend exhibition openings and performances, and, most important, contribute to the MCA's financial support fund. The last commitment may be fulfilled in different ways. Trustees are expected to contribute to the museum's annual fund; the average is $16,000 for each of the approximately fifty board members. They also participate in various fund-raising events and are asked to "introduce friends who will expand [the] fund-raising base." Basically, a trustee either gives money, helps the MCA get it, or gets off the board.[3] In return, trustees benefit from personal relationships with curators, who may from time to time advise them on purchases for their private collections.

In 1989, Oliver-Hoffmann became the MCA board president. At the time, there was talk of his making a significant financial donation as well as a gift of about a hundred artworks from his family collection. While the gift of artworks never materialized, Oliver-Hoffmann made a lead pledge of $5 million (the second largest among about 400) toward the new MCA building.

The beginning of Oliver-Hoffmann's chairmanship coincided with a restructuring of the museum's line of power. The chief operating officer (COO) post sat vacant during the first two months that Oliver-Hoffmann was chairman. It marked the first time that the chairman was not also the acting chief operating officer. Kevin Consey was eventually named COO and almost immediately there were tensions between the two men. Oliver-Hoffmann had reservations about the speed at which Consey was building his development staff. Oliver-Hoffmann wanted to proceed with caution, while Consey wanted to get the new building up and running as quickly as possible. All of Oliver-Hoffmann's objections to the board fell on deaf ears, as they supported Consey. At the end of his term in 1991, the Oliver-Hoffmanns stopped attending MCA functions. It was understood in the art circles of Chicago that they were deeply hurt by the MCA's lack of support and that they could no longer support an institution showing such fiscal imprudence.

THE OLIVER-HOFFMANN FAMILY

Paul Hoffmann and Camille Oliver met as teenagers and married a few years later. Their friends remember them as always being a happy, functional couple, which helps to explain the hyphenated surname that Paul adopted before it became fashionable. The early careers of both were in law. Camille became one of the first female lawyers in the Illinois state attorney's office. Paul was an assistant to the former chairman of Montgomery Ward. He also served for a brief time as a municipal judge.

In the late 1960s, Camille experienced serious health problems that forced her to give up practicing law. Instead, she dedicated herself to pursuing her dreams, two of which were to raise horses and to collect works of art. Paul turned his attention to real estate development during this period and was promptly successful with his investments. A trip to New York's Museum of Modern Art in the early 1970s turned their collecting interests to contemporary artists. Camille once told an art magazine that it's no fun being an art collector. "It's heartbreaking," she said. "I take one trip to New York and deplete my acquisition budget for the entire year."[4] By the 1980s, their extensive modern art collection was recognized by the MCA, prompting the museum to invite Paul to be part of the board.

While Paul was chairman of the MCA Board of Trustees in 1990, he made the first pledge toward constructing a new home for the museum. He signed a letter of intent and agreed to pay $5 million by June 30, 1997. He also agreed that the commitment would be binding on both his and his wife's estate if the pledge were not completed during their lifetime. Soon after, problems arose between the Oliver-Hoffmanns and the MCA. In the January 15, 1998, edition of *The Washington Post,* Mrs. Oliver-Hoffmann refers to the many conflicts that occurred during that time, problems that neither she nor her husband ever made public in an attempt to not damage the MCA's public image. Paul remains a member of the MCA's board by virtue of his past chairmanship, but he no longer attends board meetings.

ART AND THE FASB

Since 1973, the Financial Accounting Standards Board (FASB) has been the designated organization in the private sector for establishing standards of financial accounting and reporting. Those standards govern the preparation of financial reports. The FASB is officially recognized as authoritative by the Securities and Exchange Commission and the American Institute of Certified Public Accountants. It is independent of business and professional organizations. Decision making follows steps of due process that allow for public commentary and revisions.

The mission of the FASB is to establish and improve standards of financial accounting and reporting for the guidance and education of the public, including issuers, auditors, and users of financial information.[5] To accomplish its mission, the FASB acts to

1. Improve the usefulness of financial reporting by focusing on the primary characteristics of relevance and reliability and on the qualities of comparability and consistency.
2. Keep standards current to reflect changes in methods of doing business and changes in the economic environment.
3. Consider promptly any significant areas of deficiency in financial reporting that might be improved through the standard-setting process.

In 1995, a change by the FASB called for all nonprofit groups to record pledges as income at the time they are pledged.[6] Until this change, nonprofit organizations could recognize conditional promises-to-give as revenues or gains when the conditions on which they depend were substantially met. Substantially meeting the conditions was the major problem, as the *when* of the "event" was always open to interpretation. Some organizations recognized the pledge immediately, others when some of the pledge had been honored, and others not until the full amount had been received. So until the FASB change, organizations were free to recognize a contribution at any point along the line.

While stating that it had considered the possible effects on donor perceptions, the FASB concluded that donors and other users of nonprofit financial statements need information about promises-to-give to make informed decisions about resource allocation to those organizations. The FASB's desired goal was to force these promises to be reported as faithfully as possible without "coloring the image it communicates for the purpose of influencing behavior in any particular direction."

Ed Able, president of the American Association of Museums in Washington, D.C., which represents more than 8,000 institutions, points out that when museums record pledges as income, they will be obligated to write them off as bad debts if the pledges are not honored. The museum, thus, looks good in the year it records the pledge, but bad in the year it must write it off. The risk of being thrown into deficit situations is complicated because of this FASB ruling.

THE LAWSUIT

On December 31, 1997, the Museum of Contemporary Art filed suit in Cook County Circuit Court (Illinois) to recover $5 million from the Oliver-Hoffmanns. The suit states that on November 26, 1990, Paul Oliver-Hoffmann, an MCA trustee and, at the time of the pledge, Chairman of the Board, offered a lead pledge to begin the campaign to endow and operate the MCA's new building. Mr. Oliver-Hoffmann, on behalf of his wife and himself, made a written pledge to donate a total of $5 million, to be paid in full by June 30, 1997. The deadline came and went and the museum had not received any payments toward that pledge. From 1991 until 1997, letters of thanks combined with requests for payment were sent to the Oliver-Hoffmanns. None of these were answered.

In a press release dated December 31, 1997, Penny Pritzker, Chairman of the MCA Board of Trustees, expressed her disappointment in the unhonored pledge. She pointed out that, although the museum is "financially strong," $5 million is a significant amount of money that could be used to fund a wide range of programs. About the lawsuit, she said:

While we are reluctant to pursue this course of action, the MCA Board of Trustees has a responsibility to the museum, its supporters, and the community at large. We have always expected to receive the pledge, and have relied on its payment in planning our future. By taking this action, we are managing the museum's financial affairs professionally and appropriately.

DISCUSSION QUESTIONS

1. Who are the principal stakeholders in this conflict, and what's at stake for each of them?
2. Identify the critical issues in this case. Which seem most important from the museum's point of view? Which seem most important from the viewpoint of the Oliver-Hoffmann family and other museum patrons?
3. If you were negotiating on behalf of the museum to resolve this matter, what approach would you have taken? What's the MCA's *best alternative to a negotiated agreement*?
4. Could all of this have been resolved without resorting to legal action? Since a lawsuit is about a win/lose situation for each party involved, who stands to lose the most in this case?
5. What role does the news media play in this case? Is publicity a good thing or a bad thing for the museum?
6. Can the relationship between the Museum of Contemporary Art and the Oliver-Hoffmann family be repaired? If it were your task to mend that relationship, how would you go about it?

Endnotes

1. Neil Cossins, "Reform More Crucial Than Cash," *Management Today,* March 1997, 5.
2. Nicky Robertshaw, "Gifts That Keep on Giving: Museum Shops Help Close Revenue Gap," *Memphis Business Journal,* June 9, 1997, 6.

3. Alan Artner, "$5 Million Pledge Foundered in Power Feud," *Chicago Tribune,* January 11, 1998.
4. Mark Brown, "Art Museum Sues Couple Over Pledge," *Chicago Sun-Times,* January 1, 1998, 1.
5. From the FASB home page: http://www.fasb.org.
6. Tom Moores, "Accounting for Contributions," *The Ohio COA Journal,* 53, no. 3 (June 1994): 8.

Source: This case was prepared from personal interviews and public sources by Research Assistants Richard J. Wallen, German Riveiro, and Jack Ledbetter under the direction of James S. O'Rourke, Concurrent Professor of Management, as the basis for class discussion rather than to illustrate either effective or ineffective handling of an administrative situation. They acknowledge the assistance of Maureen King, Director of Public Relations for the MCA, for her invaluable assistance in the preparation of this case.

DEERFIELD HOSPITAL SUPPLY, INC.

BACKGROUND NOTE

Diane Jackson is the new operations manager of the Distribution Center for Deerfield Hospital Supply, Inc., a mid-size, non-union healthcare company located in the upper Midwestern United States. The Distribution Center is a $40-million-a-year operation that employs fifty people, including fifteen minorities (African-American, Asian, and Hispanic) and eighteen women in the workforce. Four of the minorities are female.

Jackson, a twenty-five-year-old college-educated woman, was transferred from another operations position in the company to fill this position because of some serious performance problems in the Distribution Center that had resisted previous attempts at improvement. The Center had experienced a very high level of defects (nearly 400 per month) as well as a high rate of errors among orders taken from client hospitals. Jackson accepted the assignment knowing that top management would expect her to improve the performance of the Distribution Center in a relatively short period of time.

Jackson's first few weeks on the job were revealing, to say the least. She discovered that the five supervisors whom her predecessor had selected to lead the Center's workforce had little credibility with the employees. They had each been selected on the basis of their job seniority or their friendship with the previous manager.

The workforce was organized into three categories. *Pickers* identify supplies by code numbers in the storage area, remove packaged items from the shelves, and sort them into order baskets. *Drivers* operate forklifts and electric trucks, moving baskets and boxes of supplies to different locations within the Distribution Center. *Loaders* transfer supplies onto and off of the forklifts and delivery trucks.

Jackson found that her employees were either demoralized or had tough, belligerent attitudes toward management and other employees. Part of the problem, she soon learned, was a lax approach to background checks and prior job references. Five employees were convicted felons, two of whom had been imprisoned for violent assaults on their victims. The previous manager had made all of the hiring decisions by himself without bothering to check the applicants' references or backgrounds.

Jackson soon discovered that it was not unusual for employees to settle their differences with their fists or to use verbally abusive language to berate people who had offended them. Her predecessor had unintentionally encouraged these disruptive activities by staying in his office and not being available to the other workers. He had relied largely on his discredited supervisors to handle their own disciplinary problems. Before long, the Center employees felt they could handle their own affairs in any way they wanted, without interference from management.

THE LOADING DOCK INCIDENT

While sitting in her office one morning, planning to make several policy changes to improve the efficiency of the Distribution Center, one of Jackson's supervisors entered and reported that two of the loaders had just gotten into a heated dispute, and the situation on the loading dock was very tense. The dispute was between Edwin Williams, a Black male employee, and Buddy Thomas, a White male employee, and focused on which radio station to play on the loading dock sound system. Williams is the only Black employee who works on the loading dock. The company's policy permits employees to listen to music while they work, and, in recent years, workers have considered listening to music to be a benefit that improves their working conditions.

Williams insisted that he couldn't stand to listen to the country-western music that Thomas preferred to play. For his part, Thomas claimed that Williams's rap music was offensive to him and made working conditions difficult. An emotional and angry argument developed between the two men over their choices in music, and each yelled racial slurs at the other. Neither the company nor the division had a policy governing the choice of music permitted in the workplace. Apparently, whoever arrived at work first chose the music for the day.

Both Thomas and Williams were known as tough employees who had previous disciplinary problems at Deerfield Hospital Supply. Thomas had been incarcerated for eighteen months prior to being hired by the company. Jackson knew that she should take immediate action to resolve this problem and to avoid a potentially volatile escalation of the conflict. Her supervisors told Jackson that, in the past, the previous manager would simply have hollered at the two antagonists in the conflict and then departed with no further action.

Jackson's objectives in resolving the conflict included the establishment of her own control in the workplace. She knew that she would have to change "business as usual" in the Distribution Center so that employees would respect her authority and would refrain from any further unprofessional conduct.

RESOLVING THE PROBLEM

In determining the most appropriate solution to the situation that Diane Jackson faces, you may wish to consider these questions:

DISCUSSION QUESTIONS

1. What are the most important issues Jackson faces today? Which is most critical?
2. Can you identify the cause of the conflict?
3. What should Jackson do to settle the conflict? Should either or both of the employees be punished for their behavior?
4. What can Jackson do over the long term to ensure that incidents such as the one described in this case are less likely to occur?
5. What role (if any) do gender, ethnicity, or age play in this situation?

6. What can Jackson do to develop a group of supervisors who can provide the support she requires and who can properly direct the work of the employees in the Distribution Center?

7. How important is communication in this case? What should Jackson do to improve the quality of communication in the Distribution Center?

Source: This case was prepared by Kay Wigton with the assistance of James S. O'Rourke, Concurrent Professor of Management, as the basis for class discussion rather than to illustrate either effective or ineffective handling of an administrative situation. Personal and corporate identities have been disguised.

GOODYEAR TIRE AND RUBBER COMPANY

EVALUATING SALARIED EMPLOYEES

For the first time in his career, Merwyn Strate, finance and accounting manager, flat-out refused to obey a corporate directive: "I felt I was being forced to do something I knew was wrong, and I had to either shut up and do it, or resist and be dealt with."[1]

After twenty years of working at the Goodyear factory in Lincoln, Nebraska, he knew he had a good team. Three of his twelve employees truly excelled, and the other nine were solid and hard working and completed everything he asked of them. Management told him, nonetheless, that he had to give two of them "A's," eight of them "B's" and two of them "C's" in their annual performance evaluations.[2]

One C is a black mark against someone's name that never fades; a "scarlet letter," said one former employee.[3] A C employee is "stuck," meaning he can't even transfer much less hope for a promotion or bonus.[4] Upon getting their second C, employees are asked to clean out their desks immediately. For a person who had proudly worked for Goodyear for decades, being told he was a low performer and then marched by a security guard past his colleagues to the parking lot was the most humiliating moment of his life.[5]

COMPANY HISTORY

Goodyear Tire and Rubber Company was founded in Akron, Ohio, in 1898 as a producer of bicycle and carriage tires, horseshoe pads, and poker chips.[6] Over the next century, the world's largest tire company had grown to employ 96,000 people worldwide with plants in twenty-six countries. Today, Goodyear is a leading producer of vehicle belts and hoses, industrial chemicals, and tires (sold under the Dunlop, Kelly, and Goodyear brands). The company, whose stock is traded on the New York Stock Exchange under the ticker symbol "GT" and held by 27,000 investors, reported 2001 revenues of $14.1 billion.[7] Today, Goodyear's strategic business units include North American Tire; Goodyear European Union; Goodyear Eastern Europe, Africa, and Middle East; Goodyear Latin America; Goodyear Asia; Engineered Products; Chemical Products; Off the Road Tires; and Aircraft Tires.[8]

GOODYEAR CULTURE

Goodyear's corporate motto is "Protect Our Good Name."[9] On November 6, 1915, the president of Goodyear, F.A. Seiberling, announced the company slogan in the *Saturday Evening Post*.[10] In depicting the role of Goodyear as an employer and a producer, Seiberling claimed this credo "makes thousands of men happier in their work and more faithful to it."[11] Seiberling helped institute a culture at Goodyear that has been described in recent times as traditional and paternalistic.[12] People join the company and expect to work there until they retire, and promotions nearly always occur from within. As Goodyear President Robert Keegan noted in a company newsletter in the summer of 2002, three-quarters of salaried employees are age forty or older.

During 1999 and 2000, Goodyear leadership underwent a transformation. A new CEO joined the firm, along with a new COO/President, General Counsel, CFO, and others. At the same time, the senior management team, comprised of individuals with substantial experience at the company, was reshuffled through the retirement of key officers and major managerial and organizational changes.[13] This cultural change was part of a general effort to revitalize Goodyear with "new blood,"[14] in the words of one senior executive at the time. This shift in human resources strategy coincided with the departure of Mike Burns, Senior Vice President of Human Resources, who announced his retirement in 1999 after thirty-four years of service to the firm.[15] Effective January 31, 2000, the company named W. James Fish, former Executive Director of Human Resources Customer Operations at Ford Motor Company, as Goodyear's Senior Vice President of Global Human Resources.[16] Among the innovations Fish brought was Ford's 10-80-10 performance evaluation system for salaried employees.

EMPLOYEE EVALUATION PRACTICES

Employee evaluation practices are influenced by an organization's industry, size, and objectives. Performance appraisal is widely considered a necessary means to assist in organizational and personnel development as well as salary, retention, and promotion determinations. Most major firms—certainly Goodyear's peers—have formally documented employee evaluation processes. A variety of methods exist for employee evaluation and appraisal, including essays, critical incident, forced distribution, trait/behavior checklists, linear scales, and management-by-objectives.[17]

For many years Goodyear had used a cascading objectives evaluation method, in which general corporate strategies drove division strategies, which, in turn, drove departmental strategies, and on down to the deliverables for individual work groups.[18] At Goodyear, employees were rated according to whether they had achieved the specified objectives established with their managers at the start of the year. This approach has known shortcomings, the most important being compliance. If managers do not hold their employees accountable for achieving their stated objectives then the system breaks down.

The ABC 10-80-10 evaluation method is a forced distribution policy. Forced distribution requires managers to rank employees relative to one another with an approximate bell curve distribution. Each employee within a specified group is assessed, for example, as "exceptional," "average," or "below average." Those employees receiving an exceptional ranking are promoted or receive accelerated compensation while those receiving a below average ranking are warned and earmarked for improvement. (Employees faced termination upon receiving their second C ranking. Goodyear provided an appeals process by which employees could have their evaluations reviewed.)

The hope of Goodyear's forced distribution was to challenge leniency on behalf of managers, and it assumed that increased competition among employees would improve productivity. Forced distribution is intended to aid managers in the identification of both above and below average performers, for reward or termination, respectively. Former General Electric CEO Jack Welch, considered a champion of forced distribution, first introduced the 20-70-10 program at GE in 1996.[19] Welch is quoted in a letter to GE shareholders as saying, "Not removing the bottom 10%

early in their careers is not only a management failure but false kindness, as well as a form of cruelty, because inevitably a new leader will come into a business and take out that bottom 10% right away, leaving them sometimes midway through a career stranded and having to start over somewhere else."[20] GE credits much of its operational efficiencies and productivity to the 20-70-10 program.

Critics of forced distribution argue that its universal application unfairly punishes members of small or superior units while advancing mediocre members of underperforming units. Lawyers representing minority groups have contended that forced rankings lead to subjective judgment that allows for personal bias or targeting of specific protected groups.

Forced distribution practices, colloquially known as "rank and yank,"[21] have existed for decades.[22] An estimated 25 percent of *Fortune 500* companies use forced distribution.[23] Ford Motor Company launched its 10-80-10 campaign in 2000, and, when faced with the prospect of the first layoffs in its history, Sun Microsystems adopted a similar program in 2001.[24] Other organizations employing a forced distribution policy include Microsoft, Hewlett-Packard, Conoco, and Cisco Systems.[25]

Even the strongest proponents of this evaluation method, however, recognize that the implementation may prove difficult. Since 1999, class action lawsuits charging discriminatory evaluation practices have been filed against Microsoft, Ford, and Conoco on behalf of African-Americans, women, older workers, and U.S. citizens, respectively.[26]

IMPLEMENTATION OF ABC

The ABC employee evaluation plan at Goodyear was initiated by HR with the blessing of Goodyear's President and COO,[27] Robert J. Keegan.[28] HR produced a handbook for managers explaining the new employee evaluation and training program.[29] Department heads and managers began announcing implementation of the system as early as December 2000, continuing through the early months of 2001.[30] Goodyear's Corporate Communications group was involved only to the extent that they reported on the new evaluation system via an internal newsletter and the intranet, where the handbook and related instructional information were also posted.[31] In Nebraska, however, Merwyn Strate reported that he never received any training on how to rate his employees via the new system.[32]

PROBLEMS ARISE

From the very inception of the ABC evaluation system at Goodyear, there were signs of trouble. Employee grumbling at Ford Motor Company over a similar policy was well known, and, in February 2001, Ford was sued by AARP (American Association of Retired Persons) for practicing age discrimination, causing further damage to the policy's credibility from the outset. Among the key problems that emerged was a lack of support for the policy from middle management.[33] The policy also provoked a lawsuit by the same team who sued Ford, and, as a result, it hurt morale throughout the company.

MANAGERS

Some mid-level managers, such as Strate, resisted putting the policy into practice.[34] When the 10-80-10 ABC initiative was handed down from above, Strate passed his opinions back up the line and tried to help keep his company from making what he believed to be a mistake that would harm morale.[35]

Judy Olian, Dean of Pennsylvania State University's Smeal College of Business, who has researched the effects of HR policies, pointed out that the ABC system at Goodyear was criticized for diminishing the ability of individual managers to motivate their employees as they saw fit, according to objectives and deliverables. Additionally, forced distribution policies can result in various tactics that degrade the bottom line, such as managers who horse-trade bad grades, or who maneuver to carry unproductive employees through the year just so they can sacrifice them to the evaluation's bottom grade.[36]

Strate criticized the actual design of the evaluation as arbitrary and lacking in context and thus believed it did not map to the actual business.[37] For example, if a worker is evaluated by a quantitative output metric, but the actual operating environment is not taken into account, how fair is it to hold the employee accountable for the product? It may be, or it may not, but situational context is critical to determine which.

What Strate explained, and a senior executive at the time confirmed, is that the policy lacked buy-in from mid-level managers because it forced them to label a certain number of their employees as low performers whether circumstances warranted that or not. Because forced distribution marks "low performers" for removal, average or even above average performers could end up in the outbox, depending on the relative size and quality of their group.[38]

AGE DISCRIMINATION

The most damaging charge against Goodyear is that the policy unfairly discriminated against older employees. While the determination of the system's intentions will be left to the courts, there are a number of ways in which age discrimination can enter the evaluation system unintentionally. For example, one of the criteria by which Strate was expected to evaluate his employees was quantity of output. If one of his employees was new to the company and entitled to only one week of vacation, while another had been with the firm thirty years and was entitled to eight weeks of vacation per year, then—all else being equal—the older employee would not produce the same quantity of output as the younger worker, simply because the older employee wouldn't work as many weeks of the year.[39]

Another example is in the language used in some of the grading criteria, such as "innovative" and "forward thinking." Without any formal training on how to apply these terms, many people associate these concepts with younger people as a matter of course.[40] An illustration of this may be the case of Jack McGilvery, a chemical engineer and holder of a number of patents, including one that received approval in August 2002.[41] Nevertheless, McGilvery was one of Goodyear's "Double C"s[42] whose career ended in 2002 because of below average performance after thirty-seven years of being told his performance was fine. Also, because a C grade could be a "career-killer," some managers may have tried to distribute them to workers who they thought might have "less career left" and who they may have thought would not be hurt as badly by the grade.[43]

Although the case was sealed upon settlement, sources close to the Ford Motor Company case say the distribution of C's disproportionately affected older workers—well over 50 percent of them were given to workers over fifty years old—and, anecdotally, the Goodyear case may turn out to be similarly skewed.[44]

OTHER HR STRATEGIES

The ABC evaluation system coincided with two other directives that helped shape employees' perceptions and put additional pressure on managers' choices. The first was a series of cost-cutting measures implemented as a result of Goodyear's economic performance, combined with the fact that more experienced (and, hence, older) employees tend to cost employers more than new recruits.

The second was the "new blood" strategy, which put pressure on managers to shake up the institution with new ideas and to attract young, energetic people from the outside.[45] In the midst of pressures to cut costs imposed by a slowing economy, the only way to make room for new people was to let current personnel go. Whether or not this played a part in individual managers' decisions is unknown, but it was certainly perceived that way by some employees.[46]

MORALE

"They just don't make guys like this anymore," Megan Bonanni, attorney for the class action suit against Goodyear, said. "Loyal company men through and through. The most egregious issue here is the emotional harm they've been done."[47]

By all accounts, the policy did damage morale. Years of being evaluated in a certain way gives anyone a level of confidence in what is expected of them. When the evaluation policy at Goodyear suddenly changed, people felt betrayed, as though the rules had changed in the middle of the game. In addition, Olian writes that in cases like this, employees feel forced to be competitive with one another because they can only survive a rating review if someone else does not.[48]

In other cases, the employees try to help out their boss. When Strate resisted, his own team told him, "It's okay. You have to do this. Just pick two of us." He still refused. The pressure he received from high up was immediate and powerful. "You're not a team player," he was told. "How are we going to reach for excellence if we don't evaluate our employees?" "You're going to mess this up for all of us." "Be careful or you'll be labeled a troublemaker."[49] Strate decided it was time to pursue the Ph.D. in human resources management he'd been thinking about.[50]

THE LAWSUIT

On September 12, 2002, eight current and former employees filed suit against Goodyear in the Court of Common Pleas of Summit County, Ohio (see Table 1).[51] The plaintiffs stated that their complaint arose out of Goodyear's implementation of a performance review system for its salaried employees. The system, which they refer to as the ABC Rating System, allegedly violated Ohio's laws against age discrimination.[52] Plaintiffs alleged that "the 2001 implementation of the ABC Rating System was part of senior management's plan to reduce the number of older employees in Goodyear's salaried workforce."[53]

According to the complaint, the plaintiffs in the lawsuit each received a grade of C and were each over the age of forty. According to the plaintiffs, the company "knowingly and intentionally implemented the ABC Rating System with the conscious purpose to unlawfully discriminate against Goodyear workers over the age of 40."[54] The plaintiffs sought to represent as a class "current and former employees . . . over the age of 40 as of January 1, 2001 . . . who received at least one grade of 'C' under that ABC Rating System and . . . who have suffered harm as a result of that 'C' rating."[55]

Among the noneconomic damages, plaintiffs allegedly suffered "humiliation, mental anguish, outrage, a sense of betrayal, embarrassment, and loss of reputation."[56] The pecuniary damages allegedly included "loss of merit increases, performance bonuses, stock options, future wages, level of retirement benefits, promotability, earning capacity, and losses associated with eventual termination of employment."[57] Furthermore, receiving a grade of C stigmatized employees and "publicly reflect[ed] senior management's view that the 'C' ranked employee is flawed and a non-viable member of the management team, [with] the long-term effect of . . . profoundly and irrevocably impair[ing] the morale of those forced to suffer this indignation."[58]

CONCLUSION

Goodyear has asserted that its ABC system did not discriminate against older employees, but nonetheless on the day before the lawsuit was filed, Goodyear announced it was going to cease

Table 1   **Relationships of Plaintiffs with Goodyear**

Plaintiff/Birth Year	Tenure	Most Recent Position	Salary
Paul Jones, Jr./1943	1967–current	Senior engineer, since 1991 or 1992	$63,500
Jack McGilvery/1943	1965–May 2002	Senior compounder, since 1991	$60,000
Thomas J. Polk/1948	1972–current	Quality assurance analyst, since 1989	$48,672
Andrew Redmon, Jr./1945	1967–current	Engineer, since 1986	$50,000
Jay Sterns/1944	1964–current	Engineer, since 1986	$58,000
James C. Sykora/1946	1968–current	Senior engineer, since 1982	$71,712
Marvin Tipton/1942	1966–June 2002 (retired)	Senior chemical lab technician, since 2002	$43,000
John S. Van Hoose/1944	1970–current	Senior design engineer	$71,760

the quota requirement that forced 10 percent of evaluated employees into the bottom category. As part of an effort to address "perceptions of unfairness" regarding its employee evaluation procedures, the company intends to provide current managers with better training in how to administer appraisals. Its new system, rolled out in February of 2003, still has three rankings, and the bottom category is intended to serve as a tool in helping low performers improve or leave.[59]

DISCUSSION QUESTIONS

1. How can a firm appraise its employees effectively without ending up in court?
2. How can a performance evaluation system be used to improve performance and institute a cultural change within an organization, without damaging morale?
3. How can management improve damaged employee morale?
4. Before attempting to change a corporate culture, what do you need to understand about it? How do you know if it will accept such a change in policy? What effects can you anticipate?
5. How important is it to get buy-in from managers for this type of change? How could that have been achieved at Goodyear?
6. How can overlapping strategic objectives affect the outcome of new policies? How did they affect the outcome in Goodyear's case?
7. What are the objectives of Goodyear's performance evaluation system? Which of these do you think were achieved? Which were not? What effect do quotas have? How might you design a system that achieved Goodyear's aims?
8. What communication avenues were available to Goodyear? Could they have helped the company avoid these difficulties? What options does the company have to address the complaints and suits?
9. What should Goodyear be communicating to its shareholders regarding the suit?

Endnotes
1. Merwyn Strate, telephone interview, November 20, 2002.
2. Ibid.
3. Megan Bonanni, telephone interview, November 20, 2002.
4. Ibid.

5. Ibid.

6. http://www.goodyear.com/corporate/chistory.html (last visited November 28, 2002).

7. http://www.goodyear.com/corporate/quick.html (last visited November 28, 2002).

8. http://www.goodyear.com/corporate/sbuprof.html (last visited November 28, 2002).

9. http://www.goodyear.com/corporate/mission.html (last visited November 28, 2002).

10. Ibid.

11. http://www.goodyear.com/corporate/protect_article.html (last visited November 28, 2002).

12. A former Goodyear executive, telephone interview, October 25, 2002.

13. http://www.goodyear.com/media/pr/22091pe.html (last visited November 28, 2002).

14. A former Goodyear executive, telephone interview, October 25, 2002.

15. http://www.goodyear.com/media/pr/21921pe.html (last visited November 28, 2002).

16. http://www.goodyear.com/media/pr/21988pe.html (last visited November 28, 2002). Fish reported directly to Samir Gibara, formerly the chairman, CEO, and president of Goodyear. Ibid.

17. Jerry Jensen, "Employee Evaluation: It's a Dirty Job, But Somebody's Got To Do It," *Grantsmanship Center Magazine* (Summer 1997). Available: http://www.tgci.com/publications/97summer/EVALUATEEMPLOY.htm (last visited December 8, 2002).

18. A former Goodyear executive, telephone interview, October 25, 2002.

19. Del Jones, "Rating Systems Trigger Criticism, Lawsuits as Companies Set Sights on Growing Labor Pool," *USA Today,* May 30, 2001, B01.

20. Julie Crane, "Forced Ranking—the Right Way," FairMeasures.com, May 15, 2001. Available: http://www.fairmeasures.com/whatsnew/articles/new237.html (last visited December 8, 2002).

21. Matthew Boyle, "Performance Reviews: Perilous Curves Ahead," *Fortune,* May 28, 2001, 187.

22. Jensen.

23. Boyle.

24. Ibid.

25. Ibid.

26. Ibid.

27. Ibid.

28. Keegan left Eastman Kodak Co. to join Goodyear in 2000 as its president and COO and, beginning January 2003, will serve as Goodyear's CEO, replacing Samir G. Gibara. Timothy Aeppel, "Goodyear Says Keegan to Succeed Gibara as Chief Executive Officer," *The Wall Street Journal,* October 2, 2002, A10.

29. A former Goodyear executive, telephone interview, October 25, 2002.

30. *Jones v. Goodyear Tire & Rubber Co.,* Case No. CV-2002-09-5090, at 5 (Court of Common Pleas, Summit County, OH, September 12, 2002) [hereinafter *Complaint*].

31. A former Goodyear executive, telephone interview, October 25, 2002.

32. Strate.

33. A former Goodyear executive, telephone interview, October 25, 2002.

34. Ibid.

35. Strate.

36. Ibid.

37. Ibid.

38. Ibid.

39. Ibid.

40. Bonanni.

41. United States Patent No. 6,427,741 was issued on August 6, 2002, to Lukich et al., for "Aircraft tire."

42. *Complaint,* 8. According to the complaint, McGilvery was terminated on May 3, 2002, prior to receiving official notice of the patent's issuance.

43. Bonanni.

44. "Goodyear Sued Over Employee Review Plan," *Reuters,* September 12, 2002. Available: http://www.forbes.com/markets/newswire/2002/09/12/rtr719724.html (last visited December 8, 2002).

45. Ibid.
46. A former Goodyear executive, telephone interview, October 25, 2002.
47. Bonnani.
48. Judy Olian, "The Force in Performance Reviews," KRTBN Knight-Ridder Tribune Business News: Centre Daily Times, State College, October 20, 2002. Available: http://www.smeal.psu.edu/news/releases/oct02/force.html (last visited December 8, 2002).
49. Strate.
50. Ibid.
51. *Complaint.* The plaintiffs named in the complaint were Paul Jones, Jr., Jack McGilvery, Thomas J. Polk, Andrew Redmon, Jr., Jay Sterns, James C. Sykora, Marvin Tipton, and John S. Van Hoose.
52. The statutory law allegedly violated is Ohio Revised Code § 4112. Section 4112.02 states that "[i]t shall be an unlawful discriminatory practice [f]or any employer, because of the race, color, religion, sex, national origin, disability, age, or ancestry of any person, to discharge without just cause, to refuse to hire, or otherwise to discriminate against that person with respect to hire, tenure, terms, conditions, or privileges of employment, or any matter directly or indirectly related to employment."
53. *Complaint,* 3.
54. *Complaint,* 4.
55. *Complaint,* 16–17. Section 4112.02(N) of the Ohio Code states that "[a]n aggrieved individual may enforce the individual's rights relative to discrimination on the basis of age as provided for in this section by instituting a civil action, within one hundred eighty days after the alleged unlawful discriminatory practice occurred, in any court with jurisdiction for any legal or equitable relief that will effectuate the individual's rights."
56. *Complaint,* 4. The complaint claimed that each plaintiff and each member of the class suffered at least $25,000 in damages. Ibid.
57. *Complaint,* 4.
58. *Complaint,* 5.
59. Associated Press, September 12, 2002.

Source: This case was prepared by Research Assistants Christopher Cronin, Navid Fanaeian, and Katrina Glerum under the direction of James S. O'Rourke, Concurrent Professor of Management, as the basis for class discussion rather than to illustrate either effective or ineffective handling of an administrative situation.

SHELL OIL COMPANY AND THE BRENT SPAR

The proposed sinking of the Brent Spar became a major controversy for Shell UK and the British government in June 1995. The planned sinking of this oil platform was canceled at the last moment after a wave of protest spread across Europe expressing concern about the environmental impact of the sinking. The decision sent a shock wave through the oil industry as companies realized the potential implications of the decision for future sensitive environmental issues and the power pressure groups can exert through public campaigns of protest.

WORLDWIDE PLATFORMS

The disposal of decommissioned production platforms is a worldwide concern for oil companies. The industry estimates that 7,300 platforms are located in oceans around the world; 219 of these installations are located in the UK Continental Shelf area. The estimated cost of disposal for these platforms is around US $40 billion.[1]

The average life of a platform is contingent on its size as well as the field and reserves where it is operating. Smaller facilities are normally designed with a fifteen-year life span, while larger facilities will last approximately thirty years. However, the reserves are usually the deciding factor in a platform's life.

Once a platform has reached its economic limits and is no longer profitable, it is decommissioned and disposed of according to the regulations in effect at the time or in accordance with existing lease stipulations. It is normally up to the platform's operator to decide the best and most cost-effective method for disposal.

The decommissioning of North Sea structures is controlled by guidelines established by the International Maritime Organization (IMO) and the Oslo and Paris Convention (OSPAR or Oslo Convention). Companies wishing to decommission and dispose of a platform must submit, as part of their abandonment and decommissioning program, a comparative assessment that evaluates the practicability, risks, environmental impact, effects on other users of the sea, and cost effectiveness.[2]

The Brent Spar platform ceased operating in September 1991 after fourteen years of service. The sheer size, weight, and structure of the Spar and its unique design as a storage and transfer facility called for special consideration in terms of decommissioning. Shell completed a three-year research study of the decommissioning alternatives available to the company in disposing of the Spar. After considering the alternatives and consulting with independent authorities, Shell proposed that the best practicable environmental option (BPEO) was a deep-sea disposal operation in 2,000 meters of water off the Outer Hebrides in Northern Scotland. Shell UK submitted the final draft of the BPEO to the British government in October 1994.

In February 1995, the British government announced its intention to approve the deep-water disposal. The announcement was accompanied with a notification, as required by the Oslo Convention, to the thirteen signatory parties to the convention (twelve nation members and the European Union). A period of two months followed in which member nations could submit objections. No replies were received in this time period.

On April 30, 1995, Greenpeace responded to the announcement by boarding the Spar and at the same time commencing a campaign to protest the decision. Four days later the German Ministry of the Environment lodged a formal protest in response to the decision. This objection came as a complete surprise to the British government and Shell, having never received a response from the German government during the time period allocated by the Oslo Convention for such action.

A CAMPAIGN OF PROTEST BEGINS

Once the British government had made the decision to approve the deep-sea disposal, Shell immediately implemented plans to tow the Spar to the designated disposal location in the Atlantic. The heat, however, was being turned up in Europe, as a major campaign was underway to challenge Shell over its decision.

Greenpeace

The Greenpeace organization was the catalyst for the protest movement, which ultimately resulted in Shell's compromise decision. One article in the *Financial Times* describes the abandoning of the sinking of the Spar as one of the greatest triumphs in the twenty-five-year history of Greenpeace.[3]

The article describes the tactics and effectiveness of the Greenpeace campaign with its powerful ability to use images and life-threatening stunts to capture the world's attention. This particular campaign followed a period of internal division over the future direction of Greenpeace. The internal conflict for Greenpeace can be attributed to the dramatic drop in "causes." Peter Wilkinson, a former Greenpeace board member, is quoted in the *Financial Times* as having said, "Greenpeace now has a fleet of ships running around the oceans looking for something to do."[4]

The campaign which Greenpeace ran, however, between April 30, 1995, and June 20, 1995, was a well-orchestrated and powerful machine, which successfully achieved the desired results. The campaign took three approaches. The first involved a direct assault on the Spar by having protesters land on the platform; Greenpeace also arranged for a ship and amphibious craft to interfere with the towing flotilla. The second involved a major information campaign in Europe seeking support and sympathy for the cause, including leaflet drops and advertisements in major newspapers. Press releases accompanied with photos and images of the protesters engaging Shell on the Brent Spar made for dramatic impact with the media. The third involved a call for a major boycott of Shell products and services. The firebombing of a Shell garage in Hamburg, Germany, although not planned or associated directly with the Greenpeace campaign, was none the less a result of the call to action that was made by Greenpeace and the environmental activists who became involved in the campaign.

The European Community

The German government was the first European government to lodge a formal protest against Shell and the UK government. This protest became the catalyst for a growing storm of protest from Europe.

> *In Germany, where opposition to the plan has been greatest, the boycott of Shell gained further momentum yesterday. For the first time in many years Germany's political parties put aside their differences to unite in opposition to the dumping of the Brent Spar. It coincided with a swelling grassroots movement involving churches, trade unions, and local politicians to boycott Shell's 1,700 petrol stations.[5]*
>
> *The protest regarding the Brent Spar quickly spread throughout Europe, and an increasing number of top-level government leaders from the Continent joined Germany's condemnation of the sinking.[6] Official protests were also received from the Danish, Belgium, and Icelandic governments.*
>
> *The public clash over the Brent Spar climaxed at the G7 economic summit in Halifax, Nova Scotia, the weekend before the planned sinking was to take place. Germany's chancellor, Helmut Kohl, challenged British Prime Minister John Major over the UK's resolve to proceed with its support for the sinking of the Spar. Major was unmoved by the criticism and recommitted his government's position that the deep-sea disposal was the best practicable environmental option.*

BRITISH GOVERNMENT RESPONSE

The Department of Trade and Industry had granted Shell the initial permission to sink the Brent Spar platform in the North Sea, 150 miles west of Scotland. All technical, environmental, and legal issues were carefully examined, and the British government was satisfied that Shell had followed the appropriate procedures outlined by the Oslo Convention. As the controversy unfolded, the British government was very supportive of Shell in all of its public briefings. Many high-level

British government officials spoke favorably both of Shell and its plan to dispose of the oil platform. Tim Eggar, the UK's energy minister, personally defended Shell's proposal in both British and European newspapers. He was quoted in the London *Times* as defending Shell's decision and attacking Greenpeace for "grossly exaggerating the problem." He added that dismantling the platform on land, as protesters were demanding, would cause "very significant environmental damage."[7] Prime Minister John Major also became involved in the public debate by openly supporting the deep-sea disposal. He went so far as to engage German Chancellor Helmut Kohl in a major difference of opinion at the G7 meeting just prior to the planned sinking.

It was this major role in defending Shell that later became the cause of great embarrassment to the British government when Shell withdrew from the planned disposal.

SHELL'S RESPONSE

Shell was taken by complete surprise when the wave of protest erupted. The initial response from Greenpeace became the tip of the iceberg, as the company faced a growing level of criticism that found its way to the highest levels of European government. The *Financial Times* ran an article entitled "Shell Stunned by Brent Spar Anger" on June 17, 1995, in which it described the shocked reaction of the Shell Oil Company in dealing with the opposition to the sinking of the Spar. The article suggested that many in the oil industry felt that Shell's handling of the issue had been disastrous and the result of a lack of careful planning and sensitivity to European reactions.[8]

Initially, Shell showed little sympathy to the Greenpeace campaign and did not anticipate the media impact of the clash between the company and protesters as the flotilla began to make its way to the disposal site. There was evidence to suggest that the company also failed to plan a corporate strategy of crisis management as Shell executives around Europe failed to communicate with any sense of solidarity on the issue. The *Financial Times* reported on June 20:

> In Germany, some senior Shell officials have voiced bitterness about their British sister company, and distaste for the UK government's seemingly arrogant attitude towards the affair. It also appears that Shell did not give its employees the advance warning that could have given them a firmer grip on events. In an interview with Der Spiegel, *the weekly German news magazine*, Mr. Peter Duncan, Chairman of Shell Germany, said he first heard about the planned sinking of the Brent Spar from the media.[9]

THE DEEP-SEA DISPOSAL IS CANCELED

Shell gave in to the overwhelming international pressure and abandoned the plan to sink the storage platform only hours before it was to be sunk. Shell justified its withdrawal with the following comments on its home page:

> Shell UK aborted the operation because the Shell position as a major European enterprise had become untenable. The Spar had gained a symbolic significance out of all proportion to its environmental impact. In consequence, Shell companies were faced with increasingly intense public criticism, mostly in continental northern Europe. Many politicians and ministers were openly hostile and several called for consumer boycotts. There was violence against Shell service stations, accompanied by threats to Shell staff.[10]

THE UK GOVERNMENT RESPONDS ANGRILY

Shortly after the news, Energy Minister Tim Eggar accused Shell of abandoning three years of detailed discussion with the Department of Trade and Industry, which licensed the disposal under the OSPAR

Convention. The *Financial Times* reported that John Major had privately characterized Shell management as "wimps."[11] The prime minister was also understood to be furious with the heads of European governments who exerted pressure on Shell to reverse its decision to sink the Spar.

In retaliation to the decision, the British government informed Shell that it would not grant the company a license to dismantle the platform on land unless it was able to prove that it was a better option than the deep-sea disposal.

SHELL ISSUES AN APOLOGY
Shell officially apologized to the prime minister for the embarrassment the company's actions had caused him. Despite the apology, Shell's actions seriously damaged the reputation of the British government both at home and abroad. By abandoning its plan to sink the platform, Shell discredited the government's approval of the firm's initial plan.

THE BRENT SPAR IS TOWED TO A NORWEGIAN FJORD
With debate still raging about the decision, Shell commissioned the Norwegian certification authority Det Norske Veritas to conduct an independent audit of Spar to verify its contents and recheck Shell UK's previous inventory. Just prior to this, on July 7, 1995, Shell received permission to moor the Spar in the deep waters of Erfjord in Norway while new disposal options were considered.

TIMELINE
1976	Brent Spar becomes operational.
1991	Operation ceases.

1995	
February 17:	Energy minister Tim Eggar approves plan to sink platform
April 30:	Greenpeace activists board platform.
May 15:	Greenpeace activists defy court order to leave.
May 22:	Police and Shell attempt to board is thwarted by rough weather.
May 24:	Last Greenpeace activists give up occupation peacefully.
June 10:	Shell tries to separate platform from its anchors. Protesters and Shell workers clash.
June 15:	German chancellor Helmut Kohl criticizes Shell and threatens to bring matter before G7.
June 16:	Prime minister John Major defends Shell to Helmut Kohl and G7. Firebomb at Shell petrol station in Hamburg. Two protesters board platform.
June 19:	Eggar calls protesters highly irresponsible.
June 20:	Two more protesters landed by helicopter. Shell abandons plan to sink platform.

DISCUSSION QUESTIONS
1. What did the company fail to consider in terms of public reaction?
2. Can you describe the basic nature of the disagreement between Shell Oil Company and its environmental critics?
3. How did the lack of communication between the European divisions of Shell contribute to the problem?
4. How responsibly did Shell handle its relationship with the UK government over the issue of the Brent Spar disposal?
5. How important is it for companies to understand and anticipate the reaction and impact of interest groups? How would you have handled the situation with Greenpeace?

6. What resolution strategies would you suggest the company adopt in this case? Is the fundamental nature of the conflict in this case unresolvable?

7. Was the change of heart by Shell Oil Company a compromise with implications for other companies dealing with controversial business decisions?

Endnotes

1. Meg Lietch, "Survey on North Sea Oil and Gas – Environmental Impact," *Financial Times,* September 4, 1995.
2. Ibid.
3. Bronwen Maddox, "Rubber Suits Turn the Tide for Greenpeace," *Financial Times,* June 21, 1995.
4. Ibid.
5. Robert Corzine and Judy Dempsey, "Shell Stunned by Brent Spar Anger," *Financial Times,* June 17, 1995.
6. Kevin Brown, "Heseltine Seeks to Limit Embarrassment – Brent Spar,"*Financial Times,* June 21, 1995.
7. Michael Cassell, "Shell Pledges to Go Ahead With Dumping Oil Rig as Row Grows,"*The Times* [London], June 19, 1995.
8. Robert Corzine and Judy Dempsey, "Shell Stunned by Brent Spar Anger," *Financial Times,* June 17, 1995.
9. Judy Dempsey, David Lascelles, and Ronald Van de Krol, "Brent Spar Dents Oil Giant's Pride Rather Than Its Profit," *Financial Times,* June 20, 1995.
10. Shell Oil Company home page: http://www.shell.com (last visited June 1, 1995).
11. James Blitz and Leyla Boulton, "UK Asks Shell to Forgo Tax Breaks,"*Financial Times,* June 22, 1995.

Source: This case was prepared by Research Assistants Mark Hales, Nikolay Nikolov, and Joshua Parker under the direction of James S. O'Rourke, Concurrent Professor of Management, as the basis for class discussion rather than to illustrate either effective or ineffective handling of an administrative situation. Information was gathered from corporate as well as public sources.

B SELECT BIBLIOGRAPHY

Allison, John R. "Five Ways to Keep Disputes Out of Court." *Harvard Business Review on Negotiation and Conflict Resolution.* Boston: Harvard Business School Press, 2000.

Beebe, Steven A., Susan J. Beebe, and Mark V. Redmond. *Interpersonal Communication: Relating to Others.* Boston: Allyn and Bacon, 1999.

Costello, Daniel. "Incidents of Desk Rage Disrupt America's Offices." *The Wall Street Journal,* January 16, 2001, B1, B4.

Dana, Daniel. *Conflict Resolution.* New York: McGraw-Hill, 2001.

Dana, Daniel. "The Dana Measure of Financial Cost of Organizational Conflict." Available: http://www.mediationworks.com, 2001.

DeChurch, Leslie A., and Michelle A. Marks. "Maximizing the Benefits of Task Conflict: The Role of Conflict Management." *The International Journal of Conflict Management* 12 (2001): 4–22.

Deutch, M. "Conflicts: Productive and Destructive." In *Conflict Resolution Through Communication,* edited by F. E. Jandt. New York: Harper & Row, 1973, 156.

Donohue, William A. "Resolving Relational Paradox: The Language of Conflict in Relationships." In *The Language of Conflict and Resolution,* edited by William F. Eadie and Paul E. Nelson. Thousand Oaks, CA: Sage, 2001, 21–46.

Donohue, William A., and R. Kolt. *Managing Interpersonal Conflict.* Newbury Park, CA: Sage, 1992, 3.

Finnigan, Anne. "Different Strokes." *Working Woman,* April 2000, 42–46, 48.

Fisher, Roger, and Scott Brown. *Getting Together: Building Relationships as We Negotiate.* New York: Penguin Books, 1988.

Fisher, Roger, William Ury, and Bruce Patton. *Getting to Yes: Negotiating Agreement Without Giving In,* 2nd ed. New York: Penguin Books, 1991.

Fortado, Bruce. "The Metamorphosis of Workplace Conflict." *Human Relations* 54 (2001): 1189–1221.

Gilbert, Matthew. *Communication Miracles at Work.* Berkeley, CA: Canari Press, 2002, 228.

Hymowitz, Carol, and Rachel Emma Silverman. "Can Workplace Stress Get Worse?" *The Wall Street Journal,* January 16, 2001, B1, Column 2 and B4, Column 3.

Isenhart, Myra Warren, and Michael Spangle. *Collaborative Approaches to Resolving Conflict.* Thousand Oaks, CA: Sage, 2000, 4–10.

Jehn, Karen A., and Elizabeth A. Mannix. "The Dynamic Nature of Conflict: A Longitudinal Study of Intragroup Conflict and Group Performance." *Academy of Management Journal* 44 (2001): 238–251.

Kelly, Joe. "Make Conflict Work for You." *Harvard Business Review,* 48 (1970): 103–113.

Levine, John M., and Leigh Thompson. "Conflict in Groups." In *Social Psychology: Handbook of Basic Principles,* edited by E. Tory Higgins and Arie W. Kruglanski. New York: Guilford Press, 1996, 745–776.

Littlejohn, Stephen W., and Kathy Domenici. *Engaging Communication in Conflict.* Thousand Oaks, CA: Sage, 2001.

Mastenbroek, Willem F. G. *Conflict Management and Organization Development.* Chichester, England: Wiley, 1993.

McCorkle, Suzanne, and Janet L. Mills. "Rowboat in a Hurricane: Metaphors of Interpersonal Conflict Management." *Communication Reports* 5 (1992): 57–67.

McNatt, Robert. "The List: Desk Rage." *BusinessWeek,* November 2000, 12.

Muir, Clive. "Can We All Get Along? The Interpersonal Challenge at Work." *Academy of Management Executive* 14 (2000): 143–144.

Munduate, Lourdes, Juan Ganaza, Jose Peiro, and Martin Euwema. "Patterns of Styles in Conflict Management and Effectiveness." *The International Journal of Conflict Management* 10 (1999): 5–24.

Putnam, Linda L. "Communication and Interpersonal Conflict in Organizations." *Management Communication Quarterly* 1 (1988): 295.

Rahim, M. Afzalur. *Managing Conflict in Organizations,* 2nd ed. Westport, CT: Praeger, 1992.

Ramsey, Robert D. "Peacekeeping in the Workplace: How to Handle Personality Clashes Among Employees." *Supervision* 58 (1997): 6.

Ruzich, Patricia. "Triangles: Tools for Untangling Interpersonal Messes." *HR Magazine,* July 1999, 129.

Sherif, Muzafer, O. J. Harvey, B. Jack White, William R. Hood, and Carolyn W. Sherif. *The Robbers Cave Experiment: Intergroup Conflict and Cooperation.* Middletown, CT: Wesleyan University Press, 1988.

Stone, Douglas, Bruce Patton, and Sheila Heen. *Difficult Conversations.* New York, Viking, 1999.

Thomas, Kenneth W., and W. H. Schmidt. "A Survey of Managerial Interests with Respect to Conflict." *Academy of Management Journal,* June 1, 1976.

Van Slyke, Erik J. *Listening to Conflict: Finding Constructive Solutions to Workplace Disputes.* New York: Amacom, 1999, 5.

Volkema, Roger J., and Thomas J. Bergman. "Conflict Styles as Indicators of Behavioral Patterns in Interpersonal Conflicts." *The Journal of Social Psychology* 135 (1995): 5–15.

Wall, James A., John B. Strak, and Rhetta L. Standifer. "Mediation: A Current Review and Theory Development." *Journal of Conflict Resolution* 4 (2001): 370–391.

Wilmot, William W., and Joyce L. Hocker. *Interpersonal Conflict,* 6th ed. New York: McGraw-Hill Higher Education, 2001, 41.

INDEX